Maine's Remarkable Women

REMARKABLE AMERICAN WOMEN

Maine's Remarkable Women

Daughters, Wives, Sisters, and Mothers Who Shaped History

Second Edition

Kate Kennedy

Down East Books

In celebration of my mother,
Nancy Elliott Kennedy, 1915–2013

Down East Books

An imprint of Rowman & Littlefield

Distributed by NATIONAL BOOK NETWORK

Copyright © 2016 by Rowman & Littlefield

British Library Cataloguing in Publication Information Available

Library of Congress Cataloging-in-Publication Data Available

ISBN 978-1-4930-2322-6 (paperback)
ISBN 978-1-4930-2323-3 (e-book)

∞™ The paper used in this publication meets the minimum requirements of American National Standard for Information Sciences—Permanence of Paper for Printed Library Materials, ANSI/NISO Z39.48-1992.

CONTENTS

————•••————

CANADA

MADAWASKA

Square Lake

CARIBOU

FORT FAIRFIELD

AROOSTOOK COUNTY

QUEBEC

St. John River

Eagle Lake

Chamberlain Lake

▲ *Mount Katahdin*

HOULTON

NEW BRUNSWICK

Chesuncook Lake

Moosehead Lake

Flagstaff Lake

Kennebec River

Wyman Lake

DOVER-FOXCROFT

INDIAN ISLAND

RANGELEY LAKES

PHILLIPS

SKOWHEGAN

BANGOR

ORONO

Andoscoggin River

FARMINGTON

NEW HAMPSHIRE

LINCOLNVILLE BEACH

✴ AUGUSTA

SHAKER VILLAGE

LEWISTON

ROCKLAND

Penobscot Bay

NORTHEAST HARBOR

BRUNSWICK

BATH

Matinicus Rock

Sebago Lake

Casco Bay

Robinhood Cove

PORTLAND

ALFRED

SCARBOROUGH

NORTH ATLANTIC OCEAN

S. BERWICK

N

0   *100 kilometers*

0   *100 miles*

MAINE

Contents

INTRODUCTION

As I ready this second edition of *Maine's Remarkable Women* for the publisher, I'm also readying myself for winter. It's October now—still bright with orange and yellow and red—but winter waits close by. Soon—a week, two weeks—there'll be a killing frost. Plants that summered on the deck and the front stoop, alfresco, now jockey for position inside. Maple and oak logs are stacked in the woodshed, last year's creosote scoured from the chimney. According to the *Portland Press Herald* weather page, we've lost over four hours of daylight since June, and we'll lose two and a half more before the winter solstice.

Winter is much on my mind when I think of the fifteen Maine women whose lives fill these pages. One of them, Tante Blanche, saved her small community of Madawaska, on the border with Canada, during the terrible blizzard of 1797. Knowing that her neighbors, scattered in remote cabins in the woods, were starving, she strapped on snowshoes and set off into the blinding snow. Behind her she dragged a sled full of life-sustaining supplies. Without her bravery, Madawaska would have perished.

Tante Blanche's people were Acadians expelled from Nova Scotia by the English. In the wilderness of northernmost Maine, she and her family at last could make their living as farmers, in peace. She was an immigrant, as were the other fourteen women whose short biographies I've compiled—except for one, Penobscot Indian Florence Nicolar Shay. For millennia, her ancestors inhabited Maine's forests in winter, and come spring, canoed its rivers down to the ocean. Their once-vast territory has now shrunk to a few islands in the Penobscot River.

Even the writer Sarah Orne Jewett, with roots extending deep into southern Maine, had family who originally "came from away." This is also true for Maine's temperance activist and social reformer Lillian M. N. Stevens, as well as for sportswoman Cornelia "Fly Rod" Crosby, daughter of Mainers from the little town of Strong.

I've added two new biographies to this second edition, those of Toy Len Goon and Marguerite Yourcenar. At first glance, these women couldn't be more different. Toy Len was an illiterate peasant from southern China who operated a hand-laundry in Portland. Marguerite Yourcenar, a resident of Mount Desert Island, was a French-speaking writer and intellectual. But they, too, were immigrants. First-generation.

Near the winter solstice in 1921, Toy Len Goon finally arrived in Portland with her husband, Dogan. Theirs had been an arranged marriage. How strange it must have seemed—the unfamiliar language and customs, the food, the cold—for a young woman raised in the warm, green Pearl River Delta. And yet she embraced this new life in America, which began in December's darkest days.

It was during another December, some thirty years after Toy Len came, that Marguerite Yourcenar sat working on a manual portable typewriter in her drafty farmhouse on Mount Desert Island. She'd only recently moved in. A sometime visitor to the United States, she'd left France on the eve of World War II. After the war, she stayed. That December night in 1950, wrapped in a shawl, she finished the last pages of her novel *Memoirs of Hadrian*, which would be hailed as a masterpiece.

I'm a person "from away" too, a transplant to Maine, though I've lived here full-time for some thirty-eight years and before that spent a few weeks each summer on an island in Casco Bay. Once a thin-skinned Californian, I've come to love winter—its bare-boned trees and gleaming snowfields and quiet. But it's not easy. Sometimes I forget that the lessons it teaches are the very ones I need: resilience, contemplation, a dash of derring-do.

In a few weeks October will end. Soon enough we'll be shoveling snow and chipping ice off the steps. When it's near zero, the deck planking will boom like ice on a frozen lake. Winter is beautiful and wild. And it will pass, as Rachel Carson reminds us. Marine biologist, conservationist, and author of *The Sea Around Us* and *Silent Spring*, Carson also had enduring ties to Maine. "There is something infinitely healing in the repeated refrains of nature," she wrote, "—the assurance that dawn comes after night, and spring after winter."

In whatever season these fifteen biographies find you, whether in Maine or elsewhere, I hope they pique your interest. Maybe you'll be struck by the many different ways these remarkable women forged meaning for themselves and those they loved. Maybe you'll marvel at the lives of your mothers and grandmothers, your sisters, friends and neighbors, living or dead, and want to know more. Maybe you'll feel wonder, as I do, at the curious, hallowed mystery at the center of our days.

MARGUERITE-BLANCHE THIBODEAU CYR

———•◦•———

(1738–1810)

Tante Blanche: The Mother of Madawaska

In 1797, violent winter storms flung snow and sleet against the logs of an isolated, rough-hewn cabin in northernmost Maine. Snow devoured carefully stacked woodpiles and mounded over small, canvas-covered windows. It seethed like sand under the plank door. Alone inside, fifty-nine-year-old Tante (Aunt) Blanche—healer, midwife, pioneer—fed logs to the fire and prayed. Christened Marguerite-Blanche Thibodeau, Marguerite was called "Tante Blanche" by family, neighbors, and friends as a sign of both affection and honor. True to her nature, she didn't dwell on her own plight; instead, her thoughts traveled across snow-swept fields and woods into other isolated cabins. There, painful scenes awaited her mind's eye: Members of the small, tightly knit community of French-speaking settlers—some her own children and grandchildren—were slowly dying of starvation.

Twice in her lifetime, Tante Blanche and her family had been expelled from Nova Scotia and New Brunswick by colonial British troops, and they'd wandered for years, searching for a place to live in peace. With backbreaking work, they had carved a new colony out of the wilderness on the banks of the St. John River (part of Maine's present-day boundary with New Brunswick, Canada). But now it wasn't war that endangered them. For two years in a row, fall floods and killing frosts had decimated their crops. In 1797—the Year of the Black

Carving of The Arrival of Tante Blanche *by Maine artist Claude "Blackie" Cyr*
Photo by Steve Young

Famine—two inches of snow fell in early September so that there was pitifully little to harvest. The settlers had no reserves, and the faraway government of New Brunswick had not yet helped with supplies. Anticipating disaster, some families abandoned their log cabins and traveled down the St. John River toward Fredericton. Most, however, decided to stay. They had spent years buffeted by war; what they desired above all else was to farm their own lands in peace.

It was a winter scoured by deep privation. At first, the pioneers lived on small game and whatever wild herbs they'd managed to gather. But even those food sources quickly ran out. Soon the last milk cow was slaughtered and eaten, the last boiled wheat licked from bowls. In desperation, a group of men set off to hunt moose, caribou, bear, deer, rabbit—whatever animals they could find in the snowy forests and along the frozen river. Among the hunting party was Joseph Cyr, Tante Blanche's husband.

After the men left, it began to snow in earnest. For eight days and nights, a blizzard raged. Many women, already sick with malnutrition, could not take care of themselves or their babies. Tables lay bare. Cabins grew colder and colder since tending a fire required a strength they no longer possessed. Children wailed, their bellies filled only with air. And still the hunters did not return.

Snowbound in her own cabin, Tante Blanche pondered all of this. Blessed with robust good health, she herself did not get sick, but she felt the full weight of responsibility for those less fortunate than she. Tante Blanche was a leader in her settlement, endowed with a natural aptitude and interest, and trained through years of experience to prepare home remedies and to help women in childbirth. Related to many settlers through birth or marriage, she couldn't just stand by and watch their dreams—and her own—expire.

She was a devout Roman Catholic who'd prayed for her community's deliverance, but prayer was not enough: She needed to take action. And so she did. First, the search for any stores of wheat and barley she might have overlooked, any stray potatoes, bits of cured meat, or uneaten root vegetables. These she bundled into pockets and leather pouches. Then she gathered every piece of warm clothing she could spare. She took down her snowshoes, strapped them onto her boots, and headed out into the storm, dragging behind her a heavy wooden sled, loaded with provisions.

The wind blew so hard it was difficult to find her way. She could barely even see the sled or the bear-paw prints her snowshoes made before they too were swallowed up. At times, earth and sky felt like one: stinging white, and bitter, bitter cold. For hours she tramped over hills, through heavy forest, across cleared fields where frozen crops lay buried under tons of ice and snow. At each cabin, she stopped to offer help. Depending on what was needed, she delivered bits of meat and grain, homemade herbal medicines, or furs to use as blankets. From the cabins of wealthier settlers, she begged any supplies they could spare, which she then distributed to the next desperate family.

Most of the cabins were single rooms made of round logs, caulked with moss, then covered with birch bark. Using her healing skills, she nursed settlers too sick to move. Inside some homes, an infant or a grandparent had already died of starvation. Here Tante Blanche stayed to lay out the dead and to pray with grieving families; then she cooked for them and urged them to eat. Along her route, she also carried intangibles as important as food: hope, faith, and health.

At last, after eight days, the snow let up and the hunters struggled back. So terrible had been their ordeal that one of them had died from exposure and another was near death. But they brought meat, and the Madawaska colony was saved. For her own brave efforts in saving the community, Tante Blanche was hailed as a hero.

By the time Marguerite-Blanche Thibodeau was born in 1738 at Beaubassin (now the city of Amherst, Nova Scotia), France and England had been fighting off and on for more than one hundred years. The prize: possession of North America. The daughter of Jean-Baptiste Thibodeau and Marie LeBlanc, Marguerite grew up immersed in French traditions. She spoke the French of her ancestors, attended Mass at the local Catholic church, and helped with farming and household chores. Her family's homeland, called "Acadia" and ruled by France, had been a vast territory that included the present-day Canadian provinces of Nova Scotia, New Brunswick, and Prince Edward Island, as well as parts of Quebec and the State of Maine. Although the Treaty of Utrecht, signed in 1713 at the end of Queen Anne's War, had officially granted all of Canada to England—including Acadia—this seems to have had little direct effect on Marguerite's childhood, in spite of her family's having had to swear nominal allegiance to England.

However, in 1755, when she was seventeen, Marguerite's relatively stable world turned upside down. In that year—during the French and Indian War—the British demanded that Acadians strictly abide by the terms of the forty-two-year-old Treaty of Utrecht. This meant signing a new oath of allegiance, not only swearing loyalty to King George II but also agreeing to take up arms against any French settlers who might threaten English authority. Many Acadians, including Marguerite's father, refused to do this.

The British reprisal was swift and brutal. Marguerite's family, along with approximately six thousand other men, women, and children, were forced from their homes. Colonial British troops, posted in New England, deported some of the Acadians to American colonies farther south. Families were separated—women from their husbands, fathers from their children—and all of their property was confiscated. Some Acadian settlements, such as Grand Pré, were burned to the ground. Families were terrorized, and the churches, houses, and farms they'd struggled to create were destroyed. And so began years of displacement and wandering. A real-life survivor of this violent upheaval, Marguerite lived many of the events dramatized by Maine poet Henry Wadsworth Longfellow in his tragic romantic epic about the Great Expulsion, "Evangeline," published in 1847. Marguerite's grandfather, René LeBlanc, was the notary public of Grand Pré, whom Longfellow's poem immortalized.

In 1755, Marguerite and her family fled north to a small Acadian settlement on the southern shore of the St. Lawrence River, called St. Louis de Kamouraska, about one hundred miles from Quebec City. In 1760, Marguerite married Joseph-François Cyr, also from Beaubassin. Three years older than Marguerite, Joseph was one of eleven children— two daughters and nine sons—of Jean-Baptiste Cyr and Ann-Marguerite Cormier. His family had known the same heartache and trauma as hers. Marguerite and Joseph shared not only an abiding, pragmatic love but a common culture and history. Their first child, named Marguerite Cyr, was born in May of 1761 at St. Louis de Kamouraska. A son followed a year and a half later, in November of 1762. But tragedy struck in February of 1763 when both children died within two days of each other from an unidentified illness. In spite of these terrible losses, life moved on, and Marguerite gave birth to three more sons: Joseph in June of 1764; Firmin in April of 1766; and Jean-Baptiste in 1767.

Because of sporadic harassment from the English, Marguerite, her husband, and his extended family kept searching for land to cultivate far from any colonial conflict. They settled in Ekoupag (now Maugerville, New Brunswick), up the St. John River from Fredericton, in wilderness territory. Here they farmed rich land on the river. Here also Marguerite's youngest son, Jean-Baptiste, died in early childhood. In 1770, Marguerite gave birth to a daughter, Théotiste Marie, and two years later a son, Pierre Hilarion, was born. Of her seven children, born over an eleven-year span, only four lived into adulthood. For mothers on the frontier, hardships were many; surely the untimely deaths of children must have been the worst.

In 1783, at the end of the American Revolution, more political trouble erupted for Marguerite and her family. Settlers from the thirteen American colonies still loyal to the British crown found themselves unwelcome in the new United States, and they emigrated to southern New Brunswick and Nova Scotia. Governor Carleton of Nova Scotia confiscated Acadian farms, including those of the Cyrs. In 1784, he granted these lands to members of the Second Battalion of Volunteers of New Jersey as well as to a regiment of American Dragoons. Acadians' petitions for the return of their farms were ignored. They had no choice but to abandon their most recent settlement and move on, yet again.

In 1784 and 1785, Marguerite's husband, eight brothers-in-law, and father-in-law wrote to the Governor-General of Canada requesting land grants in the Madawaska Territory. Each head of household eventually received two hundred acres and some supplies to forge yet another settlement. Old Jean-Baptiste Cyr, by this time in his late seventies, bowed by hardship and injustice, is said to have walked his farmland in Ekoupag one last time before leaving it forever. "My God!" he cried, "Can it be true that there is no place left on earth for a cayen [Acadian]?"

In all, twenty-four families asked for land a mile and a half below the Great Falls on the St. John River. In June of 1785, Marguerite saw her new land for the first time. What she found was rich, hilly country, much of it blanketed by tall trees, with mountains rising in the distance. Tall grass and wild hay covered much of the marshy lowlands, good feed for the animals that were to arrive that fall, sent up from Ekoupag. When she first set foot on the southern bank of the St. John, Marguerite was forty-seven years old. She and Joseph, some of their surviving children, and her husband's family were all starting over.

That first year, they pooled their belongings, helped each other clear land, and planted potatoes along with a few acres of wheat. In the winter, the men tended trap lines and spent days at lumber camps, felling trees which they would float down the St. John once the ice thawed. English shipbuilders along the coast eagerly awaited the tall straight trees for use as masts for sailing ships. In March and April, the settlers boiled down water-thin sap to make maple syrup. There was no wool in the early years of the colony: All clothes were made from fur and leather. During the summer the colonists, using oxen, cleared acres of forest, and they cultivated crops for export, as well as for their own needs. They grew enough wheat and barley to ship some down-river to Fredericton, where the grain market was brisk.

In spite of occasional boundary disputes between New Brunswick and Quebec—as well as the United States—over who controlled the Madawaska Territory, life was fairly peaceful and prosperous for Marguerite, far better than it had been closer to the seat of the British colonial government. All four of her remaining children married between the years 1791 and 1795, and she was soon a grandmother. Even before her heroism during the Black Famine, Marguerite was well known as both a midwife and a healer. By all accounts, she was a formidable woman, strong in body and character.

Thomas Albert, in his book *The History of Madawaska*, wrote:

> *When all of Tante Blanche's works of mercy became known, she became the focus of a universal veneration that bordered on adoration. She was believed to cure the sick, remove curses, find lost objects, reconcile enemies, and bring good luck. Her greatest asset was bringing the most hardened sinner back to a most exemplary life of piety. Her severe rebukes—and if these did not suffice, the threat of her formidable fist—were enough to change the most habitual drunkard, who feared her more than the bishop.*

Tante Blanche's husband, Joseph Cyr, died in 1803 or 1804. At the end of her own days, she was living in another St. John Valley settlement, Van Buren, where she died on March 29, 1810, at the age of seventy-two. Tante Blanche was buried across the river in the Catholic parish church at St. Basile (now part of New Brunswick, Canada). This would have been an almost unheard-of honor for any layman; for a woman it was an unprecedented homage.

Many of the St. John Valley's Franco-American residents still speak French as their first language and can trace their ancestry back to Tante Blanche and even beyond, to villages in France. To honor and preserve its bicultural heritage, Madawaska has "French days" when shopkeepers, town employees, and regular citizens are urged to speak their mother tongue. The region still celebrates Acadian festivals and each summer hosts huge Franco-American family reunions.

Downriver from Madawaska, in nearby St. David, the 1969 Madawaska Centennial Log Cabin, now named the Tante Blanche Historic Museum, houses artifacts from colonial days, donated to the Madawaska Historical Society. Just behind the museum, on the banks of the St.

John, is the site where the original Acadian settlers first crossed over into the new world they would finally call their permanent home, thanks to Tante Blanche's formidable heroism and charity—and perhaps strong fist.

For generations the oral history of Tante Blanche's deeds has been passed down from grandparent to grandchild in the St. John Valley. By birth and by marriage, she was an actual aunt to many young Acadian colonists. To everyone she was an honorary aunt, or, as she's sometimes called, "la vraie mère de Madawaska," the true mother of Madawaska. Marguerite-Blanche Thibodeau Cyr, a true daughter of political, cultural, and religious turmoil, displaced time and again, managed to transcend the tragedies visited upon her, transforming her life into an enduring symbol of generosity and strength.

KATE FURBISH

—•●•—

(1834–1931)
Botanic Artist in the Garden of Maine

It was a cool fall morning in 1882, and the trees of Aroostook County in northeastern Maine blazed with red and yellow leaves. Here in the wilderness, far from any city, Kate Furbish was collecting plant specimens, alone. She hadn't found anyone to go with her, but there was nothing unusual about that. Often this tiny, forty-eight-year-old woman tramped through marshes and across mountains by herself and without a thought, in search of new wildflowers, ferns, trees, mushrooms— whatever the natural world would offer up. She especially liked watery places and the plants that grew there, from pitcher plants to sundews and leather leaf.

On this particular morning, Kate was headed toward a large pond she hadn't yet explored. While climbing a wet ravine, she was delighted to find iron pyrites embedded in the surrounding slate. Using a hammer and chisel she carried in a basket on her back, she stopped to chip off several pounds of the brassy metallic crystals. These she put in the basket, along with the tools, her lunch, an insect net and bottles, and a vasculum—a box for holding newly collected plant specimens.

Soon the bank grew very steep. Kate was so focused on reaching the pond, though, that she never considered turning back. First she lifted the basket over her head and placed it above her on the bank, not far

Kate Furbish Kate Furbish Collection, George J. Mitchell Department of Special Collections & Archives, Bowdoin College Library, Brunswick

from her top leg. Her lower leg balanced on a fallen tree. Just as she pushed off, the rotten wood gave way and her whole leg was buried. Above her, the basket. Below her, sharp rocks. As she wondered how to free herself, the basket and its contents fell down, hitting her face and shoulder, and clattering into the ravine.

By this time, Kate hurt all over, but there was no one to turn to but herself. Summoning her strength, she tried to leap by throwing her weight on her free leg and then springing up. Unfortunately, the earth crumbled even more. Now she was buried up to her waist. While she rested for a short time, she planned her escape. Finally, with great effort, she managed to extricate herself. Then, after gathering up the contents of her basket, she climbed the bank again and hurried on to the pond. Eleven hours after she'd left that morning, she returned to the home where she was boarding, delighted at having found a new sedge—a square-sided marsh grass.

Catherine Furbish was born on May 19, 1834, in Exeter, New Hampshire, the hometown of her mother, Mary Lane Furbish. Her father, Benjamin, was a native of Wells, Maine. When Kate was less than a year old, the family moved to Brunswick, Maine, where they remained. Kate was the eldest and the only girl among five brothers, only three of whom lived past infancy. Her father owned a hardware store in Brunswick. He also manufactured tin and stoves and was something of an inventor, intrigued by new manufacturing and technological devices. At his store he sold mowing machines and wheel rakes, as well as fruit trees and tomato plants he'd raised from seed.

Brunswick was a lively place to grow up, a thriving town of about four thousand and a business and cultural hub on the Androscoggin River, only a few miles from Merrymeeting Bay and the Atlantic Ocean. Bowdoin College attracted thinkers and doers to Brunswick. The poet Henry Wadsworth Longfellow and its future president, Franklin Pierce, both attended Bowdoin while Kate was growing up. Harriet Beecher Stowe, whose husband taught at the college, wrote *Uncle Tom's Cabin* there. In the years before the Civil War, Brunswick was in fact a center for two important movements: temperance and abolition.

Although Kate soaked up the varied influences around her, the natural world drew her even more strongly. Her father encouraged her interest in nature on long walks around Brunswick. And no doubt she spent hours with her younger brothers, exploring fields and forests. Her father was active in town life, in particular the schools, which were among the best in the state. Kate finished her formal education at a private seminary or girls' high school in Brunswick. From December 30, 1844, to April 19, 1845, her father paid three dollars for her tuition, with an extra dollar added for Latin. As was true for many women of her time and class, Kate's education was a genteel one—more decorative than useful—and included painting and French literature, both considered appropriate for young women. She even took painting lessons in Paris and Boston.

In 1860, however, when Kate was twenty-eight, her life took a remarkable turn. After attending a series of botany lectures in Boston, given by George L. Goodale, a Maine native and later a professor of botany at Harvard, she was seized by a passion for science. No passing fancy, this was an enduring and serious devotion. After returning to her family's home in Brunswick, she began what would become her life's work: collecting, classifying, and drawing the plants of Maine. Her painting took on new significance, too. Up to that point, although she enjoyed it, it had been a leisure-time hobby, engaged in when more pressing family matters or social events didn't occupy her time; now it became her way of recording her discoveries.

The nineteenth century saw great advances in the natural, observational sciences. Many of these contributions came from amateurs. Nowadays, we think of amateurs as dabblers, not serious scholars, but in the 1800s the word carried its original French meaning: lovers, people who do something for the joy of it, not for money or fame. Surely that describes Kate Furbish's interest in plants.

During the Civil War, Kate spent most of her time in Brunswick. She helped the war effort by rolling bandages, but most of her time from late April through October—the growing season in Maine—she walked the countryside nearby, collecting plants and drawing them. The area around Brunswick had a rich diversity of plant habitats: mountains, hills, bogs, shorelines, lakes, forests, and meadows. She explored them all eagerly. In 1862, George Goodale, the botanist whose lectures had so inspired Kate, finished his survey of all of Maine's known flowering plants. His collection was housed at the Portland Museum of Natural History. This caused great excitement in the plant world since Maine's flora had not been well documented. In 1866, however, the building burned down, destroying all scientific evidence of his work. Perhaps that loss helped to fuel Kate's work in the coming years.

After the war, Kate's life took on a particular rhythm, summer and winter. Although still based at her family's home on O'Brien Street in Brunswick, she in fact spent most of the growing season traveling. County by county, she collected, identified, catalogued, and drew or painted Maine's flowering plants. Most winters she lived in Boston, where she attended lectures, visited family members and botanical colleagues, and fleshed out sketches she made in the field. First she would gather plant specimens and either draw them on the spot or take them home to draw later. Because these plants wilted quickly, she often worked late into the night—after a day spent in the field—capturing the color, the look, the peculiar aspects of each specimen. Many she preserved by drying and pressing. Sometimes she'd dab color onto her sketch while the blossom was at its freshest. Once she'd captured that particular hue, she could go back later and paint in the whole flower. Her medium was water-based paint, the pigment suspended in gum arabic. This made the colors rich and glowing.

Even for her time, Kate was considered small—but only in height, not in force of character. She had a strong profile, square shoulders, and what many observers called a clear-eyed, penetrating gaze. The year 1870 saw all of Kate's strength of character and finely tuned skills reach their zenith. She was thirty-six and living in Brunswick with her aging parents, both of whom were ill, but that spring and summer she was a whirlwind, collecting and painting more specimens than at any other time in her life. She didn't seem bothered by the long hours spent hiking into almost inaccessible places; she didn't complain about mosquitoes, mud, or heat.

By this time, because of the careful attention to detail in her water-color paintings and tireless field explorations, botany experts were beginning to notice Kate. In fact, she earned the respect of well-known naturalists such as Asa Gray and Sereno Watson. Another naturalist, George Davenport, would become one of two important and lasting professional friends. George was a Boston businessman with a family, and he was passionate about ferns. He and Kate wrote letters, exchanged plant specimens, and helped each other identify unknown samples. Davenport acted as both adviser and mentor for a woman without formal affiliations to any university or botanical society.

The year 1873 was a painful one for Kate. Within a month of each other, both of her parents died. On May 19, she wrote, "At 7:30 a.m. I left the home of my life." Although she'd inherited enough money to live independently, she'd lost her sense of security and family. Only teaching and nursing were open as professions for women of her class and time. Also, the Civil War had killed many men in her generation, so there was no real chance for marriage either. Kate's closeness to cousins on her mother's side helped to ease her grief, and she spent most of that year and into the next visiting family in Delaware.

Early in 1875, with the help of her brother John, who still lived in Brunswick, Kate found a new home. It was on Lincoln Street, in the center of town—nothing grand, just a modest white frame building, but it belonged to her alone. Most of the second floor she turned into a combination of bedroom and studio. Here, day after day, she worked at botanic paintings at her easel in a sunny window. Here also she stored her growing collection of herbarium sheets, with specimens pressed and carefully identified. Kate's Brunswick identity had always been rooted in being a daughter, and then an orphaned daughter. Gradually, however, she came into her own: a mature, independent woman, active in science and art.

In the spring of 1880, Kate was thrilled to at last be traveling in "the Aroostook," Maine's wild northeastern county, home to many unusual plants. While in Orono, outside Bangor, a staging area for her trip, she boarded with the family of Merritt Fernald. Although just a boy, Merritt was already a botanical prodigy. He would go on to work at Harvard's herbarium and eventually teach botany there, and he would become Kate's second lifelong close professional friend.

From Orono, Kate rode the train to Mattawamkeag and then traveled by stage to Fort Fairfield in eastern Aroostook County. She spent two summers in the wilds, gathering plants. Now known for its potato fields, Aroostook was then a vast, largely untouched region of boreal forests, bogs, and lakes on the Canadian border. Two of Kate's plant discoveries bear her name: *Pedicularis furbishiae*, a wild snapdragon, also called wood betony; and *Aster cordifolius L. var. furbishiae*. Merritt Fernald himself named the aster for Kate, describing her as a "distinguished artist-botanist . . . who, through her undaunted pluck and faithful brush, has done more than any other to make known the wonderful flora of 'the Garden of Maine.'"

In 1908, after thirty-five years traveling through the state county by county, Kate bequeathed her 1,326 drawings and paintings to Bowdoin College. These were bound into fourteen leather folios, twenty inches by sixteen and a half inches, still on view at the library. Even now, more than a hundred years after she painted them, the watercolors are still vibrant, each plant alive in its own particularities, its own personality. Kate did not think of herself as a decorative artist but rather a "botanic artist," whose mission was to record the special qualities of leaf, flower, stem, twig, fruit, and seed. These illustrations, often combining pencil and watercolor, are remarkable for many reasons: Kate's desire was to capture the essence of the particular specimen she held in her hand, not to draw a generic sample, so petals droop, leaves twist and curl.

Kate was a complex, interesting woman. On the one hand, she'd been brought up to value manners, social convention, and appearances; on the other, her nature seemed much more direct and strong willed, since she burned with the flame of a personal quest. Sometimes, her independent ways put her in conflict with the expectations of the time, and her single-minded pursuit of botany raised some eyebrows, but she persisted.

At the age of forty-nine, a year after her solo adventures in Aroostook, she took a grand tour of Europe. In a journal entry from Paris, dated September 16, 1883, she noted her ongoing struggle with the French woman with whom she boarded, who thought that whenever Kate went out exploring, she ought to have a male companion—in this case an elderly French gentleman. "'Tis talk, talk, talk, while I want to see, see, see," she wrote, "and I am going to see and think for, and by myself, having proved that a day amounts to more spent alone. I can ask any other Frenchman a question at a proper time as well as he, they all know I am an American, a tourist, and no lounger; and if these gray-hairs and hollow-cheeks are not sufficient to keep me out of harm's way, the more's the pity."

In 1895, Kate helped found the Josselyn Botanical Society of Maine and was its president from 1911 to 1912. Until she was quite old, she attended its annual meetings. Often she left younger members panting behind her as she led excursions into the field. She published articles in the *American Naturalist* and occasionally gave lectures, but the folios were her main focus.

Because of her long and close association with Merritt Fernald, Kate gave her collection of dried plants to the New England Botanical Society. It is now housed at the Gray Herbarium at Harvard and numbers some four thousand sheets. Kate was quite vigorous until the end of her life, though she often complained of headaches and neuralgia. She spent her last years in Brunswick and Freeport, continuing to collect plant specimens and adding final touches to the folio paintings, which she referred to as "my children." She died of cardiac hypertrophy in 1931, at the age of ninety-seven.

In 1976, Kate Furbish gained unexpected new fame. At the time, the Furbish lousewort was believed to be extinct, but while searching for endangered species in preparation for the building of the Dickey-Lincoln dam and reservoir in Aroostook County, scientists found a number of the wild snapdragons growing along the banks of the St. John River. "Save the Furbish lousewort" became a rallying cry for environmentalists, concerned about the loss of plant and animal life in that region.

Because of the Furbish lousewort, as well as other endangered species, the Dickey-Lincoln hydroelectric project was slowed and then stopped altogether; 88,000 acres of northern Maine wilderness were saved from flooding. This area might serve as a lasting memorial to the woman who dedicated herself to honoring Maine's plant riches, from lowly dandelion to endangered wild snapdragon. But it was Kate Furbish herself who wrote the most fitting description of her own life's work. In a 1909 letter to William DeWitt Hyde, president of Bowdoin College, she summed it up this way:

> *I have wandered alone for the most part, on the highways and in the hedges, on foot, in Hayracks, on country mail-stages (often in Aroostook Co., with a revolver on the seat) on improvised rafts, . . . in rowboats, on logs, crawling on hands and knees on the surface of bogs, and backing out, when I dared not walk, in order to procure a coveted treasure. Called 'crazy', a 'Fool'—and this is the way that my work has been done. The Flowers being my only society, and the Manuals the only literature for months together. Happy, happy hours!*

ABBIE BURGESS GRANT

(1839–1892)

Lighthouse Keeper

I can depend on you, Abbie!" lighthouse keeper Samuel Burgess called out to his daughter as his dory, *Provider*, headed away from tiny Matinicus Rock. It was January 19, 1856—a dangerous time of year to sail the twenty-five miles to Rockland, on the mainland, but the family's situation was dire. Usually a government supply cutter dropped off winter supplies in September, but a series of bad storms that fall had prevented any landings. Without more food, the Burgess family would starve. Without more whale oil, the twin light towers would go dark and lives might be lost as ships wrecked on treacherous rocks and shoals.

Abbie stood waving until the dory was just a speck, then she clambered back up the cobblestone beach. Her father had left her in charge, not only of her family but of the lighthouse itself. Although Abbie was only sixteen, she was tall and strong. Her mother, Thankful Burgess, was an invalid, so Abbie was used to cooking, doing housework, and caring for her little sisters, Esther, Lydia, and Mahala. She already knew how to tend the lighthouse lamps. Each evening at sunset, she and her father would climb the narrow spiral stairway to the lamp room, where a circular shelf of Argand lamps made a horizontal row. With their hollow wicks, these lamps were especially designed to burn brighter and with less smoke than conventional ones. Still, whale oil created a lot of smoke and a terrible stench when it was heated.

Painting of Abbie Burgess Courtesy of *Lighthouse Digest* magazine

Abbie and her father lighted each lamp—there were a total of twenty-eight, fourteen in each light tower. In bad weather, they kept an all-night vigil to make sure the lamps continued to burn. At daybreak, they snuffed the lights, cleaned the glass chimneys, filled the lamps for the following night, and polished the reflectors behind the lamps, which focused and intensified the beams.

When Samuel Burgess sailed for the mainland, the sea was calm, the barometer steady. But soon a terrible nor'easter shook the Rock. Quickly, the temperature dropped below zero. Hurricane-force winds howled so loudly that the family had to shout to be heard, and waves crashed violently against the house. Night after night, Abbie shuttled between the two light towers. Several times she dared to climb out on the catwalk so that she could remove sleet from the windows. One week passed, then another. Thankful and the three younger girls grew more and more frightened when there seemed no relief from the fierce winds, waves, sleet, snow, and rain. Matinicus Rock was practically under water. Huge boulders rolled and shook with each breaker thundering across it. At one point, Abbie dashed outside to rescue her hens from the coop she'd made in the rocks.

The stone house and the light towers stood steadfast, but now water began leaking under the kitchen door. During one particularly savage raging, the original wooden house, which had been her parents' bedroom, tore to pieces and blew into the sea. So much water entered the house that Abbie helped her mother and sisters climb up into one of the lighthouse lamp rooms to ride out the storm.

Four weeks after Samuel Burgess had left Matinicus Rock, ocean swells quieted down enough that he could return home safely, his dory filled with food, whale oil, and medicine for Thankful. Abbie's bravery was noticed by more than just her parents and sisters. Her story was featured in newspapers around the country, praising her efforts to save her family and keep the lights burning. The wives and mothers of seafaring

Rockland men created a friendship quilt for Abbie in gratitude for her part in saving countless lives. To honor her faithful service, sea captains whose ships had been warned off the reefs commissioned Revere Silversmiths of Boston to make her a silver bowl. But life went on as usual on Matinicus Rock: isolated, challenging, and—in its own harsh way—beautiful.

Abbie was born in Rockland Maine, in 1839, the fourth of nine children. Her father worked at a local mill for low wages, and it was a struggle to maintain the big family, especially since Thankful was often bedridden. During Abbie's childhood, Rockland—on Penobscot Bay— was home to a thriving fishing fleet and was a shipbuilding center for the huge, swift sailing vessels called clipper ships. Native Americans had named Rockland *Cutawamkeg*, which means "great landing place," and in the 1800s it was a busy seaport. The clipper trade was brisk along the North Atlantic coast, from Boston and Portland to Eastport and on to Halifax, Nova Scotia. Shipping lanes passed close to Matinicus Rock and Matinicus Island, six miles away, where a small fishing community lived.

When the position of light keeper at Matinicus Rock came open, Samuel decided to apply. It was a political post, but as long as Democrats stayed in office, he believed he'd be appointed. Although he was over fifty, Samuel seemed eager for this chance to improve his family's fortunes, in spite of the job's insecurity and the confining nature of living on a tiny rock way out at sea. The light keeper's salary was $450 a year, with a quarterly allowance for food and supplies: forty pounds salt pork, fifty-two pounds salt beef, one hundred pounds flour, eighty pounds chip biscuits, eleven and a half pounds brown sugar, six pounds coffee or one and a half pounds tea, five pounds rice, and two gallons dried beans or peas. It was a question of hardship and isolation balanced by the freedom of a fresh start. When the job was offered, Samuel accepted it.

The Burgesses moved to the Rock in the spring of 1853. Abbie was fourteen and probably the most enthusiastic and excited member of the family as the *Provider* set sail, laden with supplies. Only five of the family's nine children were aboard. In addition to Abbie, there were her older brother Benjy, who would be Samuel's assistant, and the three younger girls closest to her age: Esther, Lydia, and Mahala. The two oldest daughters, Miranda and Louisa, mature enough to lead their own lives, remained in Rockland, where they raised the two youngest Burgesses, Rufus and Jane, since the Rock was deemed too dangerous a place for such small children.

Samuel took charge of the lighthouses on the second Tuesday in April. On the mainland, flowers would be blooming soon and trees leafing out, but Matinicus Rock was a barren spot, without even a blade of grass. So many shipwrecks had happened on nearby reefs that President John Quincy Adams commissioned a lighthouse to be built there in 1827. That first winter, during a terrible nor'easter, the lighthouse washed away and was later replaced by twin light towers.

While the Rock itself looked desolate, it was in fact a prime nesting ground for Atlantic puffins, seabirds that never come ashore except to build their nests in shallow depressions in the rocks. Puffins mate for life and always return to the same island to raise their young. During the nesting season, they take on bright, parrot-like colors, which later fade to black and white. When Abbie lived on the Rock, it was home to seventy pairs of nesting puffins, as well as to terns, guillemots, and gulls. The waters surrounding the Rock were rich fishing grounds, full of halibut, flounder, mackerel, and cod.

The light keeper's house, in the center of the island, was bigger than the one the Burgesses had rented in Rockland. There was a huge cistern for collecting rainwater, a cobblestone washhouse, a boathouse for *Provider*, and a one-ton bell inside a wooden structure. Matinicus is the third-foggiest light station in Maine, with more than 1,700 hours of fog a year. Whenever fog cloaked the island and the lighthouses' beams were dimmed, someone would need to pull the heavy bell rope once every ten or fifteen minutes, round the clock, to warn ships off the reefs.

It became clear early on that Benjy yearned to leave the Rock and join the fishing fleet, but he stayed to assist his father. As well as tending the lights, they built a hundred lobster traps and fished them in stringers in nearby waters. Benjy often sailed back to Rockland for supplies, taking the lobster catch with him to sell on the mainland, a good supplement to his father's salary. It was Abbie's lot to do most of the domestic work at the lighthouse and to watch her younger sisters and brother so her mother could rest. Although she seemed not to complain about this, it was in the light towers where she truly felt happiest.

Since Benjy was often away, Abbie became her father's helper, showing both aptitude and keen interest from the beginning. For Abbie's mother and sisters, life on the Rock often felt confining, boring, and lonely. They talked about what they'd left behind, what they couldn't do anymore, what they didn't have: schools, libraries, parties, gardens, friends outside the family. To Abbie, however, the island offered beautiful vistas and a vast round world of sea and sky, endlessly fascinating and changeable. Eagerly, she learned how to tend the lights. No one expected a girl to do this, but Abbie had found what she loved, and she convinced her father that she was up to the task.

Soon enough, Benjy left the Rock to join a mother ship with twelve fishing dories, which sailed for Bay Chaleur, just below the Gaspé Peninsula in Quebec, Canada. Before Samuel gave his permission, however, Benjy and Abbie had to persuade him that she could handle the job of assistant keeper. Finally, Samuel relented, and Abbie took on her life's work. Not only was she strong, well-trained, and responsible enough to serve as assistant keeper, but she also helped her father lobster, then haul up the dory by hand—dressed in oilskins over her long skirts.

Part of the light keeper's job was to write in a log each day, recording weather conditions and anything remarkable that happened. During her watch in the light towers, Abbie read these logs avidly. In an entry dated June 11, 1833, one keeper had measured Matinicus Rock and "found it according to his figures 2,350 feet long, 567 feet wide, 34 $\frac{6}{10}$ acres." In January 1839, breakers over forty feet high had carried away the keeper's house, though he and his family had escaped in a dory and were later picked up by a passing schooner.

Within a few months, Samuel Burgess trusted Abbie enough that he would sail to Rockland, alone, every Monday to sell lobsters and buy supplies. He'd stay overnight and sail back the next day, which meant that Abbie was in charge of tending all the lights in his absence.

In March of 1856, officials from the Lighthouse Board visited the Rock to plan for improvements to the lights. By now, clipper ship traffic was waning. It was only a matter of time before steamships, though still expensive to run, would supplant the giant sailing ships. The Burgesses had always believed the lights shone as far as fifteen miles out to sea, but it turned out the distance was closer to nine. Plans included building a second light tower and installing Fresnel lenses to replace the old Argand ones. Now, both lighthouses would shine with brighter, more piercing beams.

In May, Abbie's brother Benjy returned to the Rock. With the decline of the clipper trade and subsequent job losses in Rockland, employment on fishing boats declined as well. Although her brother could now help their father again, it was Abbie who still lighted the lamps at night. In June, a crew installed an engine for a steam-driven fog whistle. Instead of manually ringing the bell, the Burgesses just needed to keep a fire burning under a boiler so the whistle would blow.

During that winter, stores of food and whale oil again ran very low because bad weather had prevented the supply cutter from visiting the Rock. In fact, Samuel believed his family would starve to death in just a few weeks if he didn't reprovision immediately. In spite of bad weather, he headed to Rockland, alone. When Samuel did not return, Benjy built a dory and sailed off to look for his father, as well as to get more food and whale oil. Once again, Abbie was responsible not only for her family's welfare but for the safety of mariners out at sea. A week passed. Benjy still hadn't returned nor had Samuel. The flour barrel was empty, and there were no more dried apples and raisins. Abbie rationed her mother and sisters to an egg a day, plus one cup of cornmeal mush.

At last, in March, her father and brother returned safely. A month later, construction began on new twin towers, 180 feet apart. One was 10 feet from the house; the other was 140 feet away. This meant more work for the light keeper, though a covered walkway was also created between the two towers. Brighter lamps were installed. A 24-by-26-foot frame house was built as the future home for an assistant light keeper. Samuel and Thankful moved into it, while the children continued to live in the original house.

Three years later, Lydia was seventeen and wanted to go to Boston to attend art school. Esther was sixteen and Mahala fifteen; both were eager to leave the island for a broader life. Thankful, too, was tired of living on the Rock. But Samuel and Abbie did not want to go. The 1860 election sealed the family's future: When the Republican candidate, Abraham Lincoln, was elected president, Democratically affiliated Samuel Burgess lost his job. On a trip to Rockland after the elections, Samuel urged his friend Captain John Grant to apply for the position. In turn, Grant was appointed light keeper to begin in March of 1861.

Twenty-two-year-old Abbie felt so sad at the thought of leaving the light station that her father allowed her to stay on to help the new family learn the ropes. The Grants, including three sons, were large, friendly, and robust. The mother was as vigorous as the others and enjoyed Abbie's company. The youngest son, Isaac, took great interest in the running of the lighthouses. Soon he was also very interested in Abbie herself. The two fell in love and were married the next summer. For fourteen years they stayed on the Rock, serving as paid assistants to John Grant. Abbie and Isaac's four children—Francis, Malvina, Mary, and Harris—were born on Matinicus Rock. Another child, two-year-old Bessie, died suddenly and was buried there because the weather was too severe to leave the island.

In 1875, after twenty-two years of service at the light station, Abbie moved off Matinicus Rock when Isaac was appointed keeper of White-head Light Station, also in Maine. She served as his paid assistant until they both retired in 1890. In her final letter to a friend, Abbie wrote:

> Sometimes I think the time is not far distant when I shall climb these litehouse stairs no more. It has almost seemed to me that the lite was part of myself. Many nights I have watched my part of the night and then could not sleep the rest of the night, thinking nervously what might happen should the lite fail. . . . In all these years I always put the lamps in order in the morning and I lit them at sunset. Those old lamps on Matinicus Rock—I often dream of them. When I dream of them, it always seems to me that I have been away a long while, and I am hurrying toward the Rock to lite the lamps there before sunset. I feel a great deal more worried in my dreams than when I am awake.
>
> I wonder if the care of the litehouse will follow my soul after it has left this worn-out body! If I ever have a gravestone, I would like it in the form of a lighthouse, or beacon.

Abbie Burgess Grant died in 1892 at the age of fifty-three and was buried in Forest Hill Cemetery in South Thomaston, near Spruce Head and the Whitehead Light Station. In 1945, historian Edward Rowe Snow, who had read Abbie's letter, commissioned a miniature light-house to be built—an aluminum scale replica of the one on Matinicus Rock. This he placed on top of her grave: a fitting honor for a woman who, defying the conventions of the time, spent her life lighting beacons along the rocky Maine coast.

Keepers no longer tend the lights on Matinicus Rock; the lights have been automated since 1984 and are maintained by the Coast Guard. Thanks to the National Audubon Society's Puffin Project, the seabirds Abbie so enjoyed watching—once hunted to near extinction for their colorful plumage—have returned to nest on her beloved Rock.

Lillian M. N. Stevens

(1844–1914)

Temperance Activist and Social Reformer

Lillian Stevens wasn't afraid of anything or anyone. You might not share her views on a particular issue, but you'd much rather have her fighting on your side than against you. More than one man came to find this out too late. It was midmorning, so one story goes, when Lillian appeared in the office of an elected official. As part of his duties, he was supposed to enforce "Maine's law," the statewide prohibition on manufacturing and selling alcohol, originally enacted in 1851. In fact, she knew him to be a slacker.

Lillian had a ship-of-state bearing, imposing and confident in her long black Victorian dress and bonnet. Although many of Portland's homeless women and children knew Lillian for her kindness, on this particular day her looks and manner were severe. She got right to the point: If reelected, she asked the man, would he start cracking down on the liquor traffic?

The fellow tipped his hat back to get a better look at her. Then he propped his feet up on his desk, picked up an orange, and cut it in half. Mrs. Stevens was one of those temperance ladies—he knew the type—always waving Bibles and praying for sinners, while demolishing barrels of whiskey with their sharp little hatchets. They'd already stirred up trouble, but you didn't need to take them too seriously. Without saying a

Lillian M. N. Stevens Collections of Maine Historical Society, #11076, ca. 1890

word, the man slowly ate one of his orange halves. When he finished, he deigned to tell Mrs. Stevens that what he did was none of her business.

Lillian's long skirts hissed as she turned to leave his office. "I shall make it my business," she told him, "to do all I can to defeat you." The time would come when he'd be sorry he didn't remove his hat, take his feet off his desk, and ask if she'd like the other half of that orange, she added.

That morning the official may have smirked, but Lillian kept her word: She labored mightily to defeat his reelection bid. After his loss at the polls, he at least had the good grace to apologize for his rudeness—and for his unwillingness to share his orange.

While the details of this story may have been embellished over the years, it was typical of Lillian to stand her ground. From a young age, she was not only aware of social causes but willing to put her beliefs on the line, starting with the presidential campaign of 1856, when she was only twelve. At issue was the abolition of slavery.

Because John C. Frémont, the pro-abolition candidate, was very popular in her hometown of Dover, Maine, Lillian saw a great many flags emblazoned with his name as she walked to school each day. She felt so passionately about the abolitionist cause that she sewed her own banner and stitched Frémont's name across it. To publicize her support, she stretched the banner across the road in front of her house, tying it between two tall pine trees. One day an old man, who was driving his horse and wagon into town, passed under Lillian's banner. Apparently he hated the idea of abolition so much that he pulled over, left his wagon, and started climbing one of the pines to cut the flag down. Lillian, watching from a window, quickly figured out what the man was doing. She dashed outside toward the wagon and startled his horse enough to make it bound away. The man scrambled down the tree trunk and chased after his horse and wagon, leaving the John C. Frémont banner undisturbed.

Lillian Marilla Nickerson Ames was born March 1, 1844, at the family farmhouse on the edge of the little central-Maine town of Dover (now Dover-Foxcroft). Her mother was Nancy Fowler Ames; her father, Nathaniel Ames, was a teacher. Hers was a happy childhood, spent studying at the village school and playing in nearby hills and woods with her brother and two sisters. When she was twelve, however—the same year she made the banner for the anti-slavery candidate—her older brother died. This loss turned her thoughts to religion and to caring for others.

Lillian was a slender girl with black hair and hazel-colored eyes. Her voice was low, her face composed and serious. She was an eager student who loved school. After she graduated from Foxcroft Academy in the town next door, she studied at Westbrook Seminary (now part of the University of New England) in the suburbs of Portland, Maine. Even then, Lillian impressed teachers and fellow students with her quiet authority. In *Lillian M. N. Stevens: A Life Sketch*, Lillian's daughter, Gertrude Stevens Leavitt, relates this story:

> *Once when a young woman said she was sorry for her [Lillian] because she cared more for books than bonnets, and solid study rather than social success, a classmate replied: "No one need be sorry for Lillian Ames. She will be remembered years after the rest of us are dead and forgotten. I cannot tell just why I think so, but I am perfectly sure that she will make good."*

Lillian's next venture was teaching at both the Spruce Street and Stroudwater schools in Westbrook. Although teaching was one of few professions open to women at the time, traditionally only men were hired for the winter term. Many almost-grown boys, who worked on farms or on boats during the spring, summer, and fall, attended school in the winter and were thought too big and rough for women to handle. But not too big and rough for Lillian. As one of the first women hired to teach during the winter term, she defied convention and did it handily. She was a strict, demanding teacher, and a popular one. Not only did her students learn, they liked and respected her.

In 1865, when Michael Stevens, a well-to-do salt and grain wholesaler, asked Lillian to marry him, she accepted. In that era, because married women were not allowed to teach, Lillian's decision meant the end of her teaching career. For a woman of her energy, intelligence, and need to be useful, this choice must have been a difficult one. Nevertheless, she threw herself into the role of Victorian wife, becoming a fine cook, hostess, and seamstress. She and Michael moved into his family's large brick house—built in 1803 by his father—in Stroudwater, a historic section of Portland. (The house remains in the family, now occupied by the Stevenses' great-great-grandson.)

Lillian and Michael had one daughter, whom they named Gertrude Rose. Soon, though, the wider world beyond the domestic sphere called to Lillian, and she responded. In the winter of 1873–74, news of the "Women's Temperance Crusade" stirred her activist nature. During that campaign, female churchgoers marched into Ohio saloons—or knelt outside them in the snow—to sing hymns and pray. Similar demonstrations swept the country, closing thousands of saloons in twenty-three states. Although most soon reopened, the temperance cause ignited a wildfire. Anti-alcohol groups had been agitating since the early part of the nineteenth century, but they were small and not centrally organized. Now, however, women began to unite. In November 1874, the Woman's Christian Temperance Union (WCTU) was founded in Cleveland, Ohio.

In spite of her own settled, privileged life, Lillian was very aware of problems affecting poor women and children. She believed, as did growing numbers of other women—and some men—that alcoholism was at the root of society's major troubles, poverty and domestic violence among them. Before the Civil War, some Northern white women had worked hard for abolition; now, after African-American men gained the right to vote in 1870, many of these same women turned their attention to temperance and suffrage.

During the summer of 1875, Lillian took young Gertrude to Old Orchard Beach on the Atlantic Ocean twenty miles south of Portland. Crowded into an open-air tent, they heard a speech by Frances E. Willard, a well-known educator and temperance activist. Lillian listened, spellbound, to Frances's words. Here, Lillian felt, was her calling. After the meeting, she rushed to the stage and introduced herself. The two would become close lifelong friends and colleagues.

Although Maine's prohibition law had been in effect in one form or another since 1851—due in large part to the efforts of Portland's mayor, Neal Dow—liquor could still be found. That fall, inspired by Frances Willard, Lillian organized the state's first Woman's Christian Temperance group, the Stroudwater Union, and became its first president. In 1878, she was elected president of Maine's WCTU, an office she held for the rest of her life.

Lillian's husband, Michael Stevens, shared her temperance zeal and was very supportive of her reform efforts. To make it easier for Lillian to focus on her work, they hired a governess to care for Gertrude. As president of Maine's WCTU, Lillian visited almost every town in the state, driving her beloved horse, Madge, some fifty thousand miles. For most women, belonging to the WCTU was their first experience with flexing political muscle. Lillian's example—her sense of herself as a strong and confident woman, her clarity of purpose, her willingness to stand up for what she thought was right—made her a galvanizing force, a role model, not only in Maine but around the country. Women flocked to her side.

In 1879, Frances Willard ran for president of the National WCTU, whose offices were in Chicago. Her platform embraced women's suffrage as a way to promote temperance. This double-pronged activism split the organization into two warring factions. Lillian stood by her friend, who won the election. Under Willard's leadership, "Do Everything" became the WCTU's rallying cry, as different local chapters fought for different causes, among them suffrage, labor laws, and prison reform—all under the umbrella of temperance.

At the WCTU National Convention in 1880, Lillian was chosen to serve as assistant recording secretary. She rose quickly in the ranks. By 1894, she'd become vice president at large. As Frances Willard's right-hand woman, she now traveled the country fighting the powerful liquor industry, as well as advocating for social reforms of many kinds. By 1895, the WCTU had approximately 135,000 members, making it the largest organization of American women at that time. As such, it had an early and profound influence on women's advancement toward political power.

In 1896, after the Turkish massacre of Christian Armenians, refugees from the fighting fled to France, where Frances Willard, visiting England on temperance business, heard about their plight. She sent telegrams, begging each WCTU leader to help twenty-five refugees resettle in her community. Immediately Lillian answered, saying Portland would open its doors to fifty Armenians. She met them at the docks in Portland; they'd been told to look for a woman with a white ribbon on her coat, a WCTU symbol. Lillian and other Maine union members gathered clothing and food and found housing and jobs. Some refugees may even have camped in her backyard. The first child born to Portland's Armenian community was named Willard Stevens.

While Lillian thrived as a national-level temperance leader, she also kept an eye on social problems closer to home. Her friend Frances Willard wrote that "the streets of Portland, Maine, have not a sight more familiar and surely none more welcome to all save evil-doers than Mrs. Stevens in her phaeton [carriage] rapidly driving her spirited horse from police station to Friendly Inn, from Erring Women's Refuge to the sheriff's office."

Lillian prodded her wealthy friends to be generous with their time and resources, and she led by example. Within a fifteen-year span, a total of nineteen homeless children lived at the Stevenses' house on Westbrook Street. Lillian spearheaded the drive to create an Industrial School for Girls and was a founder of the Temporary Home for Women and Children, where she spent many hours volunteering. She also served as treasurer and then president of the National Council of Women, a group that advanced women's work in education, reform, and philanthropy.

After Frances Willard's death in February 1898, Lillian became her handpicked successor as president of the National WCTU. Two years later, Lillian also became vice president of the World WCTU. As such, she organized international conventions in Boston, Brooklyn, Scotland, and Switzerland. The scope of these endeavors was breathtaking, the pace dizzying. In 1905, for example, Lillian and her assistant, Anna Gordon, traveled ten thousand miles in just nine weeks on temperance business.

During Lillian's tenure as president of the National WCTU, she grappled with many thorny issues, including friction with the National Woman Suffrage Association (NWSA). Lillian herself was a passionate supporter of women's right to vote. Even so, the NWSA asked her to stop promoting its cause. Its leaders felt that the future of women's suffrage was being jeopardized by its association with temperance and prohibition, since the WCTU had powerful enemies in both the liquor industry and in politics. It was a painful schism. Reluctantly, Lillian agreed to withdraw from the Maine Suffrage Association.

Still, under Lillian's direction, the National Woman's Christian Temperance Union acted on more than just the anti-liquor front. For example, it lobbied strongly on behalf of the Pure Food and Drug Act, which passed in 1906, and the Mann Act of 1910. The Mann Act outlawed the transportation of women and girls between states and out of the country for "immoral purposes." In her 1910 address to the National Convention of the WCTU, Lillian noted that "buying, selling, deceiving, forcing and imprisoning their victims are among the methods employed by the trade, and the terrible evil is widespread."

For her time, Lillian Stevens was an interesting crucible of unusual qualities. A product of the Victorian era, she was ladylike, a genial hostess with impeccable manners. She could also wither those who opposed her. To a twenty-first-century reader, her language of "sin" and "evildoers" may sound overbearing or moralistic, even patronizing. Undoubtedly some members of the WCTU did look down their noses at "sinners," but Lillian herself seems to have genuinely loved her fellow human beings and worked for social change. She combined her deep religious faith with commonsense practicality about how to best aid those in need. Workers at the WCTU's national headquarters in Evanston, Illinois, looked forward to her visits. Not only did they appreciate her clear, logical mind and forceful direction, they also loved her wit, her friendliness, and the excitement she brought to their cause. They fondly called her "the chieftain."

In 1911, Maine's prohibition law was challenged in a referendum vote. Lillian organized a statewide campaign in support of keeping the ban against liquor sales. When the measure narrowly passed, keeping prohibition, Lillian felt that finally the time was right to push for a national Prohibition Amendment to the Constitution. Letter-writing campaigns, fasting, prayer vigils, public speeches, parades, street meetings, rallies—all culminated in a National Constitutional Prohibition Amendment Day on January 15, 1914. That morning, Lillian attended a gathering at the First Free Baptist Church of Portland, where she gave her last speech. She ended by saying:

Some glad day the states in which today is entrenched the liquor system will rejoice that it has been abolished. Science, philan-

thropy, reform, religion, and the business world are testifying against the liquor traffic. In the light of all this we can see prohibition looming up all the way from Mt. Kineo in the east to Mt. Shasta in the west, from the pine forests in the north to the palmetto groves in the south. We verily believe that the amendment for National Constitutional Prohibition is destined to prevail and that by 1920 the United States flag will float over a nation redeemed from the home-destroying, heart-breaking curse of the liquor traffic.

Lillian did not live to see the Prohibition Amendment to the Constitution pass Congress and be ratified by forty-four states in 1919, but she had helped to lay the groundwork. While the Prohibition experiment, repealed in 1933, proved unsuccessful, her work on behalf of social justice endured.

On April 6, 1914, at the age of seventy, Lillian died of kidney failure at home, in the company of her husband, her daughter Gertrude, and her good friend and successor as president of the WCTU, Anna Gordon. Her last words were, "My full day's work is done." Gertrude nodded, then said, "And well done."

Lillian chose to be cremated and was buried in the old Stroudwater Cemetery across the street from her house. After her death, flags in Maine flew at half-mast, the first time a woman was so honored. Tributes poured in from around the world. In her memory, the WCTU presented a water fountain to the City of Portland in 1917: a bronze statue of a young girl, set on a Maine granite base. There was also a drinking trough for horses and a special basin for dogs and birds. This fountain now stands inside the glass entryway of the Portland Public Library's main branch on Congress Street.

After her mother's death, Gertrude delivered this quiet appreciation: "Mother had a cheerful smile, was a loyal friend, and most unselfish. She often said 'to love one's self last went a long way towards establishing the kingdom of Heaven in one's heart.' She demonstrated that so well. She was utterly fearless. She saw all sides of a question. She didn't talk about her religion but lived it every day of her life."

SARAH ORNE JEWETT

---•◦•---

(1849–1909)

Writer from the Country of the Pointed Firs

It was a fine June morning. Cardinals shrilled from the branches of willows along the riverbank—a bead of sound, a flash of red. Nine-year-old Sarah Jewett closed her eyes a moment to savor the sweet smell of lilacs while her father's horse and buggy swayed along the packed dirt tracks of a country road. But just as quickly her eyes popped open; she didn't want to miss a thing. Her father, a country doctor, had invited her to forego school for the day and make house calls with him, and she had jumped at the chance. Now they sat, side by side, on the seat of his buggy. Sunlight sheened off the horse's rump and warmed Sarah's dark hair.

Suddenly, Dr. Jewett reined in his horse, climbed down from the buggy, and motioned for Sarah to follow. Out of the mass of vines and tangled greenery beside the lane, he pointed to a particular shrub with twisted twigs, splayed out in all directions—witch hazel. She remembered the surprise of its feathery yellow flowers last fall, how they'd bloomed only after the leaves died back, on the coattails of a snowstorm.

Later, when they stopped at a weather-beaten farmhouse, she followed her father inside and observed everything that happened; she listened to him draw his elderly patient into conversation, noticed which herbs and medicines he prescribed. Not only did she learn about

Sarah Orne Jewett (right) with her friend Emily Tyson, 1905 Courtesy of Historic New England/SPNEA

healing during these trips, she also soaked up landscape and seascape, characters and stories—and the intricate workings of human nature.

Years later, when she'd become a well-known writer, Sarah told an interviewer, "The best of my education was received in my father's buggy and the places to which he carried me." She credited him with encouraging her to feel sympathy "for the dreams of others" and with calling "my attention to trees, birds and flowers. He urged me to tell things just as they are, and said nothing in the world is uninteresting if you only look at it long enough. In this way he taught me how to write."

Theodora Sarah Orne Jewett was born in South Berwick, Maine, on September 3, 1849, to Caroline F. Perry and Dr. Theodore H. Jewett. The middle child, she had one older sister, Mary, born in 1847, and another sister six years younger, Caroline, nicknamed Carrie. South Berwick was a small port, ten miles up the Piscataqua River from the Atlantic, in the most southerly corner of Maine. When Sarah was little, her family lived in the center of town, in a big white house belonging to her paternal grandfather; later they moved to a smaller house next door. Her grandfather had run off to sea as a boy and worked his way up to captain, then shipbuilder and wealthy merchant. Sarah's maternal grandfather was a well-to-do doctor, with whom her father had interned.

By all accounts, Sarah's formal education was erratic. She attended a "dame school" but sometimes skipped classes, suffering, she claimed, from "instant drooping if ever I were shut up in school." She also missed days because of poor health—bouts of rheumatoid arthritis—for which her father recommended lots of outdoor exercise. "I wasn't like the usual village schoolgirl," she once wrote. "I grew up as naturally as a plant grows, not having been clipped back or forced in any unnatural direction." Free to roam the town, she loved listening to old sailors' stories at the docks and the latest gossip from customers at the dry goods store. Despite spells with painful swollen joints, she became an expert horsewoman. She also learned to sail and row on the river; in winter she skated, snowshoed, and sledded with her sisters. "Wild and shy" were the words she used to describe her childhood self, yet her mother also taught her to entertain and to manage a household.

Both of Sarah's parents encouraged her to read, and she did so avidly, ranging widely in her family's library. As a girl, she wrote poetry and kept detailed journals. In her early teens, she read Harriet Beecher Stowe's novel *The Pearl of Orr's Island*, which dealt with everyday characters on a real Maine island. The rural people and places she'd come to love, she realized, were worthy subjects for literature.

In 1866, Sarah graduated from Berwick Academy, the oldest preparatory school in the state. She thought about studying medicine, but because her health wasn't robust enough, she abandoned that idea. While continuing to live with her family, she often visited relatives in Boston for parties, plays, and concerts. And always, she wrote. When just nineteen, she published her first work of fiction, a melodramatic romance entitled "Jenny Garrow's Lovers." It appeared in the magazine *The Flag of Our Union* under a pseudonym, A. C. Eliot. Another story, "Mr. Bruce," was published in the December 1869 issue of the *Atlantic Monthly*, also under a pseudonym. At her sister Mary's urging, she told the rest of her family that she was the author, though at first she regretted doing this because now the story "no longer belonged all to me."

By 1873, when she was twenty-four, Sarah was actively seeking advice from editors about how to improve her writing, in particular William Dean Howells, a well-known writer and the editor of the *Atlantic Monthly*. As much as she sought out suggestions for mastering her craft, she also had a sturdy, independent sense of her own writer's path, regardless of editors' literary taste. Artistic independence was easier for her, of course, than for some other women writers of her time since, as the daughter of an upper-middle-class family, she never had to make a living from her work and could focus on it exclusively without financial worries.

Sarah was drawn to write what she called "sketches" of country life. These emphasized creating characters rather than showcasing plots. Her aesthetic, "imaginative realism," drew from the local color movement of regional fiction but also from such writers as French novelist Gustave Flaubert, whose fiction, rooted in commonplace details, she greatly admired. Sarah was so impressed with his work that she pinned two of his quotations to her desk: "Write ordinary life as if writing history" and "The writer's job is to make one dream."

In 1877, at the urging of William Dean Howells, Sarah collected her stories about small-town life into her first book, *Deephaven*. It sold well and, in general, was reviewed enthusiastically. With her first royalties, Sarah bought a chestnut thoroughbred. "I believe I should not like Sheila half so well if she were tamer and entirely reliable," she wrote of her horse—in some ways a mirror of herself. "I glory in her good spirits and think she has a right to be proud and willful if she chooses."

By the late 1870s, Sarah was publishing stories in such magazines as *Harper's Monthly* and *Scribner's*, as well as the *Atlantic Monthly*. While she wrote about the disappearing virtues of Maine farms and coastal villages, she was also becoming part of a worldly artistic community. Her publisher, James T. Fields, and his wife, Annie Adams Fields, became her close friends. Annie was a writer, a social reformer, and a generous hostess. The Fieldses lived at 148 Charles Street, at the foot of Boston's Beacon Hill, in a large mansion, which they opened to new and established writers of the day. At dinner parties and readings—often lasting late into the night—the Fieldses created a fertile atmosphere where Sarah shared her work and ideas with such famous authors as Longfellow, Emerson, Whittier, and Hawthorne. She also came to know Matthew Arnold, Henry James, and Charles Dickens when they happened to visit Boston.

But at the heart of Sarah's fiction, as in her life, lay friendships between women, whom she portrayed as self-reliant, independent, and in charge of their own lives. Whether widowed or unmarried, these characters created a place for themselves in a world where women's futures were usually defined by marriage and motherhood. Early in her career, Sarah established a network of powerful women friends, like fellow writers Celia Thaxter and Amy Lowell, who also frequented the Fieldses' get-togethers.

When John Greenleaf Whittier once asked Sarah why she'd never married, she supposedly answered that she had "more need of a wife" than a husband. "I do not wish to be married," she wrote on another occasion. "Would you have me bury the talent God has given me? Doing this work lovingly and well is the best way I can see of making myself useful in the world." In the companion book to the film biography of Sarah Orne Jewett, *Master Smart Woman*, Cynthia Keyworth notes that Sarah was "more of a bachelor than a spinster," emphasizing the fullness and exuberance of her chosen lifestyle, her freedom from the usual constraints imposed on Victorian women.

In September 1878, Sarah's father died—her earliest dear friend and teacher. During her grieving time, she found the friendship of Annie Fields especially comforting. Less than three years later, in 1881, Annie's husband, James, also died. In the summer of 1882, the two women sailed to Europe, drawn together by their shared loss, and during that trip, they fell in love. They became life partners and champions of each other's work, as well as travel companions. In that era, such intimate, intense, and supportive relationships between two women were called "Boston marriages." Sarah and Annie were widely accepted as a couple. For the next two decades, Sarah's life took on a seasonal pattern: She spent half a year at 148 Charles Street and half a year at her family's home in South Berwick or at Annie's summer house in Manchester-by-the-Sea, Massachusetts.

When apart, the two exchanged frequent letters. Not only did they express their feelings—using many endearments and the pet names

"Pinny" for Sarah and "Fuffy" for Annie—but they recorded the details of their lives and their work. In 1883, after William Dean Howells declined to publish Sarah's short story, "A White Heron," she wrote to Annie:

> *Dear Fuff,*
> *. . . but what shall I do with my white heron now she is written? She isn't a very good magazine story but I love her. I mean to keep her for the beginning of my next book.*

"A White Heron," now one of Sarah's best-known and most anthologized stories—and an example of early environmental awareness—deals with an unsophisticated country girl named Sylvie, who chooses to protect the hiding place of a beautiful, rare heron rather than expose it to a young man from the city who wants to kill it and stuff it to add to his trophy collection.

In her novel *A Country Doctor*, published in 1884, Sarah tried to capture something of her father's character in Dr. Leslie, a kind and intelligent man who adopts a child, Nan Prince. Echoing her own childhood adventures with her father, Sarah has Nan accompany Dr. Leslie as he makes house calls on his rural patients. Nan, who runs wild in the woods, as did Sarah, decides to become a doctor herself and in the end gives up the idea of marriage and children so that she can achieve her dream. Of all Sarah's works, this was her favorite.

During the 1890s, Sarah continued to write in spite of many personal sorrows. Her mother died in 1891, as did her brother-in-law a year later. In 1894 it was her very close friend Celia Thaxter who died. Then in 1897, her younger sister Carrie passed away, leaving behind a son, Theodore Eastman, to whom Sarah was devoted.

From January to September of 1896, when she was forty-nine, Sarah's novel *The Country of the Pointed Firs* was serialized in the *Atlantic Monthly*. In November it appeared in book form. This loosely structured novel of linked stories was narrated by a woman writer from the city who spends a summer in Dunnet Landing, a place much like St. George Peninsula on the Maine coast, which Sarah and Annie had visited the previous year. Still considered a masterpiece, *The Country of the Pointed Firs* was both a critical and a commercial success, and Sarah became one of America's most popular and respected writers. The narrator is deeply changed by her encounters with the residents of the town and outlying islands, yet she keeps herself out of the way as the stories of local lives unfold. The book is full of humor, compassion, and keen insight, and its style is carefully crafted. In describing the odd character of Joanna, a woman who lives alone on an island as penance for a tragic love affair, Sarah's narrator muses, "In the life of each of us, . . . there is a place remote and islanded, and given to endless regret or secret happiness."

Sarah's 1901 book, *The Tory Lover*, a historical novel set at the Hamilton House in South Berwick, tried to portray a passionate love affair between a man and a woman. But it was much less convincing than her earlier work. After reading the novel, Henry James wrote: "Go back to the dear Country of the Pointed Firs, come back to the palpable present intimate that throbs responsive, and that wants, misses, needs you, God knows, and suffers woefully in your absence."

During that same year, Sarah became the first woman to receive an honorary degree from Bowdoin College. This honor celebrated a writing career that spanned more than thirty years and produced over 170 works of fiction. In September of 1902, on her fifty-third birthday, Sarah was thrown from a carriage, injuring her spine so badly that she never fully recovered. In December of that year, still recuperating in South Berwick, she wrote to Annie Fields:

> *My darling, you know that it goes very hard with me that I can't be with you on Christmas. We are closer than ever in love and*

friendship and belongingness, aren't we? It is wonderful with all the chances and changes of life that I have managed to have part of Christmas Day in Charles Street for twenty years without a break.

Although dizziness and terrible headaches hindered Sarah from writing fiction, she was able in her remaining years to help younger women writers, such as Mary Ellen Chase and Edith Wharton. Most significantly, she mentored Willa Cather, whom she met at Annie Fields's house in 1905. Struggling as a journalist in New York City, Willa turned to Sarah for advice and encouragement. Sarah urged her to return to Nebraska, where she'd grown up, so that she could focus on the kind of material she was driven to write.

In a 1908 letter to her young protégée, Sarah, who'd always thought of her own work as "experimental," advised this: "Don't try to write the kind of short story that this or that magazine wants—write the truth, and let them take it or leave it. . . . Make a way of your own. If that way happens to be new, don't let that frighten you." Inspired by Jewett's example and belief in her talent, Willa Cather did return to Nebraska, creating such memorable novels as *O Pioneers!*, *My Ántonia*, and *The Song of the Lark*, set in the prairie landscape she knew and loved.

In March of 1909, while staying with Annie Fields in Boston, Sarah had a stroke which left her partially paralyzed. At the end of April, she returned to South Berwick, where she convalesced in her beloved old white house on the town square. "I was born here and I hope to die here leaving the lilac bushes still green, all the chairs in place," she wrote. Her wish came true. After a second stroke, she died at home on June 24, 1909, just after the lilacs bloomed. She was fifty-nine.

In 1910, Sarah's friends established the Sarah Orne Jewett Scholarship Fund at Simmons College. It honored her women-centered stories and the great potential she saw in expanding young women's horizons.

In 1911, Annie Fields published a book of her and Sarah's letters, though her publisher insisted that she delete many of the endearments and expressions of affection, believing that society might "misinterpret" their friendship.

During the first half of the twentieth century, Sarah Orne Jewett's writing, often dismissed as "minor," was relegated to the local-color shelf, read by devotees of Maine's rural past. But in recent decades, feminist scholars have reexamined her books in a new light. In *Sarah Orne Jewett: Her World and Her Work*, critic Paula Blanchard describes her as "an unsurpassed chronicler and interpreter of women's lives."

Sarah's family home in South Berwick, maintained just as she left it, is owned by the Society for the Preservation of New England Antiquities, as is the Hamilton House, described in *The Tory Lover*. Both are open to the public.

Sarah Orne Jewett's real legacy, of course, remains her body of literary work. It is important that we remain connected to the past, she reminds us, that we treasure simple pleasures and the unspoiled bounty of nature. Sarah herself described it this way: "I fear this world is on the point of vanishing. But what a luminous beauty its sense of decay gives off!"

It's not just a long-ago world she sought to animate, however. Even today, her characters inspire readers to follow where their deepest natures lead them. "I long to impress upon every boy and girl this truth: that it is not one's surroundings that can help or hinder—it is having a growing purpose in one's life to make the most of whatever is in one's reach."

CORNELIA "FLY ROD" CROSBY

(1854–1946)

Sportswoman and Journalist of the Maine Woods

O n March 16, 1896, the Second Annual Sportsmen's Exposition opened at Madison Square Garden in New York City. Front and center at Maine's exhibit was Cornelia "Fly Rod" Crosby—noted fisherwoman, hunter, sports journalist, and enthusiastic promoter of wilderness tourism in her home state.

"Camp Maine," as it was called, took up six exhibitors' spaces. It included a cabin of peeled logs—studded with stuffed deer heads— and fish tanks full of a hundred live Maine salmon and trout. Fly Rod demonstrated fly-fishing and extolled Maine's virtues to all passersby. She wore a special Paris-inspired hunting costume designed for her by Spaulding Brothers of New York: a suit of tanned green leather, with a mid-calf skirt, matching tall green lace-up boots, and a tailored jacket, worn with a red sweater and jaunty red-and-green hat. The newspapers of the day praised Fly Rod and her daring outfit, but years later she would tell an interviewer that many women were scandalized:

> *Yes, sir, Fly Rod with her wild and wooly guides, her speaking acquaintance with the beasts and birds of the great north country, was looked upon as some aborigine! I think many were disappointed because I did not emit a warwhoop every so often.*

Cornelia "Fly Rod" Crosby Maine State Museum

What the men thought, I can't say, but I am positive the women all regarded me as a first-class freak!

More than eight thousand people each day stopped at "Camp Maine" during the exposition's six-day run. As exciting as the fish tanks, the log cabin, and lifelike taxidermy turned out to be, it was forty-two-year-old Fly Rod who proved the biggest draw. By 1896, she was a celebrity, the "Queen of Anglers." The *New York Journal* described her as "an athletic country girl, born in the state of Maine . . . as proud of her $1,000 collection of fishing tackle as most girls are of souvenir spoons or blue and white china." The Sportsmen's Exposition of 1896 was important to Fly Rod for another reason: During that short week, she made a lifelong friend, Annie Oakley, who was appearing at the exposition as a sharpshooter.

Cornelia's parents, Lemuel Crosby and Thurza Cottle Porter Crosby, both grew up in the small western Maine town of Strong. When they married they moved to nearby Phillips, where Thurza gave birth to Ezekiel in 1845, followed nine and a half years later by Cornelia Thurza, born November 10, 1854. Lemuel tried various business ventures from a starch factory to a store, where, among other things, he brokered furs trapped in the region. But his health was always poor; before Cornelia turned two, he died of consumption—tuberculosis.

Both Cornelia and Ezekiel, it seemed, inherited their father's sickly constitution. In that era, doctors advised that "delicate children" spend as much time as possible outdoors. Cornelia loved the woods and waterways around Phillips. For her, the fresh-air cure worked wonders, at least for a time. But Ezekiel didn't share her luck. In 1868, when he was only twenty-three, he, like his father, died of consumption. Cornelia, aged thirteen, and her mother were now the only Crosbys left. The bond between them remained very strong until Thurza's death in 1903.

Sometime in her teens, Cornelia inherited $600, most likely from her father. Showing levelheaded good sense—and the understanding that she'd probably need to be self-supporting—she invested the money in her own education. At the time, $600 paid for two years at an Episcopal girls' finishing and college preparatory school, St. Catherine's Hall, in Augusta, Maine. There, in the company of girls from well-connected families all over New England, Cornelia learned social graces and forged friendships that would help her throughout her life.

During much of the 1870s, Cornelia worked as a bank teller in Franklin County, not far from Phillips. She taught Sunday school at the Congregational Church and joined women's social organizations. But when her health failed, as it did periodically, she would spend months recuperating, unable to work. Sometime before 1878, she had an experience that would shape her future. She described it this way:

> *After long months of illness from a severe lung trouble, from which I was not expected to recover . . . I was carried, one June day, to the very foot of Mount Blue. . . . Here at a farmhouse I was to try the healing power of nature. A brook full of trout came laughingly dancing down the mountainside, and from there I took my first trout, with an alder pole, it is true.*

By 1878, Cornelia was fishing at mile-long Tim Pond in the Rangeley Lakes region. Instead of a makeshift pole, she used a split-bamboo rod, the gift of its maker, Charles Wheeler of Farmington. Although Rangeley Lake itself is only nine miles long, the Rangeley Lakes region is an angler's dream: 112 lakes and ponds with names like Cupsuptic, Aziscoos, and Mooselookmeguntic.

In the early 1880s, Cornelia worked as a telegrapher in Phillips. More importantly, she spent as much time as she could during the season— May through October—fishing in the Rangeley Lakes and detailing her experiences in a column for the *Phillips Phonograph*, the town's first newspaper. During that period she had relapses of her lung condition, sometimes for long stretches. In spite of that, her journalism career was heating up. By the end of October 1883, she was also Phillips's official reporter for *The Franklin Journal*, published in Farmington.

Her editor at the *Phonograph*, O. M. Moore, was the first person to call her "Fly Rod." The name stuck, and "Fly Rod's Note Book" became a popular column. Her style was chatty and humorous, much like a personal letter. She had a knack for combining her own fishing adventures—and comic misadventures—with information about where to stay and social notes about the people who ran sporting camps as well as those who stayed there.

The 1880s was a time of economic upheaval for Maine. After a decade of stable, farm-based prosperity, young people had begun leaving family farms for manufacturing jobs in the cities, and parts of the state felt deserted. To offset revenue lost from hauling freight, the Maine Central Railroad began to encourage tourism, paying Fly Rod as the state's first recreational publicist to promote the "outdoor industry." Soon a slogan she'd developed—Maine, The Nation's Playground—was known all over the country.

In the Gilded Age of the 1890s, well-to-do visitors seeking the healthy life and natural beauty Fly Rod described flocked to western Maine, often fleeing cities that the Industrial Revolution had left clogged with polluted air and water. Families stayed at wilderness camps, usually in small rustic cabins with a central lodge where they took their meals. Called "sports" or "rusticators," these "soft adventurers" hired local fishing and hunting guides whom they followed into the wilds every morning. Women as well as men loved fly-fishing, a sport of finesse rather than brute strength, and in spite of the day's fashions (including tight corsets, floor-length skirts, and high-necked gauzy blouses), they managed to take to the woods. Through her larger-than-life example and her persuasive columns, Fly Rod pioneered women's active enjoyment of nature and championed the call for less restrictive clothing:

Why should not a woman do her fair share of tramping, hunting, and fishing and ask no odds of the men? The time is past; I thank Providence, when it was thought unladylike for a woman to be a good shot or a skillful angler.

Here, in another of her columns, dated May 31, 1895, Fly Rod entertained herself and her readers by gently poking fun at a visiting "sport" while, no doubt, leaving both him and his wife eager for more:

About the most delightful angler on the Monday train was Mrs. W. P. Whitehouse, wife of Judge Whitehouse of Augusta, who for the first time had been fishing at Rangeley. . . . The Judge one morning started off with his guide and said: "Don't suppose there is some old pole, a string, and a few worms and Mrs. W. could amuse herself fishing off the wharf while I go out and get a big trout?" Coming back at night with two little trout, the Judge found his wife had amused all the camp by landing [fifteen] two-pounders.

The seasonal rhythm of Fly Rod's life was well established by the mid-1890s. She worked at banks, if her health allowed it, from November through April and did some traveling around New England, though her home base was always Phillips. Once the ice thawed on Maine's lakes, she spent her summers at various fishing camps. She was among the first to promote catch-and-release fishing. In the summer of 1893, which she described as "the happiest and best of my life," she caught over 2,500 fish. Her one-day maximum was two hundred fish—many of which she presumably released back into the water—and she held a record for most fish caught in the shortest amount of time: fifty-two trout in forty-four minutes. Fly Rod also traveled north and east in the fall for Maine's deer and moose hunting seasons, which she described in detail for her eager readers.

As Fly Rod's fame increased, so did her collection of fishing tackle, much of it donated by admirers and by companies who wanted her to mention their fishing equipment in her syndicated columns. In that sense, she was one of the first female professional athletes—like her friend Annie Oakley—with the equivalent of today's product endorsements. "I am a plain woman of uncertain age, standing six feet in my stockings," she once wrote. "I have earned my bread for a good many years doing the work of a bank clerk. I scribble a bit for various sporting journals, and I would rather fish any day than go to heaven."

During the winter of 1894, Fly Rod helped Harvard professor A. R. Sweetser organize the Greenville-Rangeley Camp, a natural history camp for boys, the first of its kind. That summer Fly Rod was in charge of excursions for the twenty-five campers from wealthy families. The next winter she busily organized Maine's contribution to the first Sportsmen's Exposition held at Madison Square Garden in May of 1895. The exhibit's centerpiece was a ten-by-thirteen-foot log cabin, called "Camp Maine Central." A taxidermist from Bangor, Maine, supplied stuffed fish and animals, and there were hundreds of photographs to whet tourists' appetites.

Fly Rod, with her imposing height, mythic skills, and personal charisma, could have easily been perceived as threatening to the men with whom she fished and hunted, and to the increasingly powerful Maine Sportsmen's Fish and Game Association, of which she was the only female member. In fact, she met with the opposite reaction. Fly Rod made no secret of her anti-suffrage point of view; she didn't believe women should vote. While this seems at odds with the way she herself freely crossed traditional gender boundaries, it did allow her to work and travel easily with men and exert influence in areas about which she cared deeply, such as conservation measures to ensure the future of fish and game. It also meant she avoided the vitriol heaped upon active suffrage fighters such as Elizabeth Cady Stanton and Susan B. Anthony.

In fact, Fly Rod's contributions to women's rights were important and lasting. In his master's thesis "Diana of the Maine Woods," March O. McCubrey notes that Fly Rod presented Maine as Edenic for women as it offered them not just a retreat from the modern world but a retreat from restrictive social prohibitions. Women, when engaged in outdoor sports, could be liberated from their restrictive clothing. In some cases, especially after the turn of the century, women organized their own activities, free from the supervision of male relatives and friends. . . . Crosby thus helped to construct an atmosphere promoting female involvement in male oriented activities, a rare occurrence in the urban world.

In 1897, the Maine Fish and Game Association hired Fly Rod as a "special agent" to increase its membership rolls. She actively lobbied the Maine legislature on behalf of a state-run system for registering Maine guides and increasing the state's Fish and Game budget to $40,000. She also continued working for the Maine Central Railroad, organizing Maine's third exhibit at the Sportsmen's Exposition in New York.

One day that week, decked out in her green leather hunting outfit, Fly Rod hosted a "pink tea" for the Women's Press Club—only pink refreshments were served that afternoon, in the shadow of the world's largest mounted moose head. Later in the week, while handing out promotional flyers, Fly Rod received a telegram stating that the "Guide Bill" had passed the legislature. She was delighted. In the future, registered Maine guides would need to buy a license for one dollar a year and file a one-page annual report. In honor of her efforts to pass the bill and as a thank-you for all she'd done for her state, she was given the very first license, though she never worked as an official Maine guide.

By now Fly Rod was busy full-time—Maine's original booster. She organized the state's entry at the Boston Food Fair, a festival of cooking demonstrations and commercial food exhibits. Like a ringmaster in her famous green suit, Fly Rod presided over "Camp Aucocisco" and its cabin, stuffed deer, and 107-pound squash. The exhibit also included her mother, demonstrating spinning, and a beautiful Penobscot young woman, Lucy Nicolar, showing how to make baskets. Fly Rod was, as usual, the main attraction.

The Fourth Annual New York Sportsmen's Exposition, which started on January 12, 1898, was also an enormous success, with increasing numbers of women attending. In the fall of 1898, Fly Rod was hired to mount a display at the Eastern Maine Fair in Bangor—another triumph. But soon after that event closed, she was admitted to Portland Eye and Ear Hospital because of an injury suffered the previous spring. While boarding a train, her skirt had caught, and she was dragged several hundred feet. Her knee was badly wrenched in the accident. Apparently, tuberculosis then attacked the injury site, which resulted in surgery and months of inactivity.

Although she was sidelined for about two years, Fly Rod kept writing and managed to do some fishing while hobbling on a crutch. For the Sportsmen's Exposition of 1901, she represented the Washington County Railroad's "Sunrise Route," which brought tourists to eastern Maine's beautiful hills and lakes. Annie Oakley dropped by the Maine exhibit every day. The two friends now had even more in common than before. Not only were they both professional athletes—women who navigated successfully in what was considered "a man's world"—but they'd also both suffered debilitating injuries, gone through surgery, and endured long, painful months in the hospital.

The year 1903 was a very difficult one for Fly Rod. Her mother—her life's companion and strongest supporter—died in February after a long illness. Doctors ordered bed rest for Fly Rod because of frayed nerves and her bad knee. Though she lived with chronic pain, she kept writing for the *Maine Woods* and other national publications throughout the decade, advocating for wildlife preservation.

As the 1920s dawned, Fly Rod, now in her sixties, suffered increasingly poor health. When, by 1926, she lost sight in one eye and could no longer fish, hunt, or hike in the woods, her spirits plummeted. She spent the spring of 1926 in St. Mary's Hospital in Lewiston, Maine, "trying to regain from a nervous breakdown and heart trouble," as she described it. Fly Rod managed to rise from her own ashes, however. Because of the kindness of Catholic health workers and friends, she converted to Catholicism and returned to Phillips, to the Rangeley Lakes, to write and enjoy nature as best she could.

In September of 1929, when she was seventy-five, Fly Rod described her daily life this way: "I am now crippled, nearly blind, and alone, living with pleasant memories of the days gone by, with gifts from friends and souvenirs from the past." But, according to one newspaper clipping, she still managed to fish the Rangeley Lakes when she was over eighty.

Fly Rod still spent her summers in Phillips until close to the end. She died on Armistice Day, 1946, a day after her ninety-third birthday, and was buried in the Village Cemetery in Strong, next to her parents and brother.

Authors Julia A. Hunter and Earle G. Shettleworth Jr. end their biography, *Fly Rod Crosby: The Woman Who Marketed Maine*, with this evocation of Fly Rod's enduring appeal:

> *She loved the life there [in Rangeley], and that love came through in her writing and her public appearances. She shared her own adventures with fishing rod and gun with her readers, and she also made a point of writing about the activities and successes of other women who came to the region for fishing and hunting, or to study or simply enjoy the local flora and fauna. Presenting herself as a woman who was an accomplished woodswoman, her message was clear: I have gone out and done this; it is wonderful; you can do it, too—come on, this is fun!*

LILLIAN "LA NORDICA" NORTON

———•◦•———

(1857–1914)

The Yankee Diva

L illian Nordica, from the western Maine village of Farmington, was a renowned operatic soprano, "America's first international diva," when an interviewer happened to ask if she did needlepoint to calm her nerves before walking out on stage. No, she answered, she couldn't knit nor could she do multiplication tables, for that matter. "But patching is my specialty," she added. "I can put on a good New England patch as well as anybody."

For all her diamonds and sapphires, three turbulent marriages, and celebrated performances in the opera houses of New York, London, Paris, Milan, and St. Petersburg, Nordica never lost sight of her practical, plainspoken Maine roots. She only lived in Farmington until the age of seven, but it remained the solid footing upon which her life of stunning vocal achievement was built; it was the one place this citizen of the world referred to as "home."

Lillian Norton, called Lillie, was born on December 12, 1857, the sixth daughter of Amanda Allen and Edwin Norton, whose ancestors had ploughed the land outside Farmington. The fifth daughter was the original Lillian, but after she died at the age of two, her name passed to the next daughter, a custom of the time called "repeating." Edwin, Lillie's father, was not well suited to farming, and debt plagued the

Lillian Norton and her poodle, Turk Hoffert/Berlin/Opera News Archives

family, but still they managed to create a rich cultural climate for their daughters, full of music, literature, and languages. Lillie's mother was the family's mainstay, a dynamo of intelligence, tenacity, and ambition. "Give me a spoon," she once said, "and I won't hesitate to dig a tunnel through a mountain."

The youngest in a large family, Lillie was used to receiving little attention and early on learned to look out for her own interests. It was her older sister, Wilhelmina, nicknamed Willie, who seemed destined for a great singing career. In 1864, hoping to improve their fortunes, the family moved to Boston. At first they tried running a boardinghouse, then Edwin turned to photography, but nothing quite worked out as planned. Always resourceful, Amanda clerked at Jordan Marsh's department store. The family pinned its hopes on Willie's extraordinary soprano voice, which she developed at the newly founded New England Conservatory. At home, the entire family sang. Lillie was forever imitating Willie's scales and vocal exercises; in fact, she became such a pest that her family paid her a few pennies not to sing.

In the fall of 1868, the Nortons were visiting cousins in Farmington when heavy rains caused flooding of the nearby Sandy River. In the wake of the flood, sixteen-year-old Willie caught typhoid fever and died. The family plunged into mourning. While Willie's death dashed Amanda's high hopes of fame and fortune, it also opened the way for Lillie. For two years Amanda grieved, almost dead to the world, then suddenly, as if for the first time, she really listened to her youngest daughter sing.

Now the family's energies focused on Lillie. She was just fourteen when her long, difficult years of operatic training began, first at the New England Conservatory, where she studied with Willie's teacher, John O'Neill. Brilliant and inspiring, O'Neill was also such a taskmaster that Lillian was the only one of his original students to last the full four years, which she later described as "stained with tears and sodden with discouragement." But she, like her mother, never gave up hope and never stopped working hard. For all of the sacrifices Lillie made, however, she also felt transcendent joy. The aria "Visi d'Arte" ("I Live for Art") in Giacomo Puccini's opera *Tosca* might describe Lillie Norton's reality too: fully dedicating herself to the gift of an amazing voice.

While Lillie dreamed of one day singing in the world's great opera houses, her feet still stayed firmly planted on the ground. In the years she studied at the conservatory, her family struggled; everyone worked just to survive. Lillie herself took a part-time job at a bookshop and spent her lunch hour walking the streets so that the other clerks wouldn't know she was too poor to afford a meal.

After graduation, Lillie, accompanied by her mother, left for New York, where she studied with Italian opera singer Madame Maretzek. By this time, two of the Norton daughters were married, and Edwin went to live with one of them. The Nortons were prepared to sacrifice even their house to further Lillian's career. To afford her continued lessons, Lillie soon was singing with Patrick Gilmore's band in Madison Square Garden. For $100 a week and expenses, including those of her mother, she joined Gilmore's tour of the West and, in 1877, traveled with him to Europe. For Lillie, singing in Dublin, London, and Paris felt like a grand opportunity, and the reviews were good.

In Paris, however, Lillie soon left the band, believing she needed to risk everything in pursuit of serious operatic training. Her schedule left little time to rest: She studied operatic acting with an elderly Frenchman, François Delsarte, and voice training with Emilio Belari, in addition to taking French lessons every day. Back in their tiny apartment, she practiced *Lucia di Lammermoor*, *La Traviata*, *Faust*, and *Aida*, sometimes six hours a day, and taught several students of her own. When Delsarte died suddenly, Lillie and Amanda left for Italy, where Antonio Sangiovanni, a great teacher at the Conservatory of Milan, agreed to teach her for free.

Sangiovanni was kind, and Lillie made great progress with her singing. She was excited about her approaching debut as Donna Elvira in Mozart's opera *Don Giovanni*; still, the work was strenuous, the hours long, their apartment cold and dank. On March 10, 1879, Lillian stood in the wings, waiting for her cue, when the audience screamed the leading prima donna off the stage. Although Lillie's own singing won the audience's approval, most of the other leads were fired and the production scratched. Then it was on to Brescia, where she sang the role of Violetta in *La Traviata*. This time her singing caused a major sensation: Every aria was encored, adoring crowds rushed the footlights, bouquets of flowers showered the stage. The next morning a string band stood under the window of "La Nordica," serenading her with *Traviata*'s overture. This was the success for which the whole Norton family had worked and sacrificed.

But success still exacted a price. Lillian and her mother weren't able to spend the summer in Farmington and Boston as they'd hoped. Edwin, who had not fully recovered after an explosion at his photographic studio, nevertheless urged his wife and daughter to stay in Europe. In spite of homesickness and financial troubles, the family remained intact; they exchanged long letters and, now, newspaper articles about La Nordica.

That fall Lillie was hired to sing ten secondary roles at the Imperial Opera in St. Petersburg, Russia. Although she'd already memorized sixteen roles, none of these was in the opera's repertoire. With only six weeks before the season started, Lillie learned all the new parts. Her performances met with such wild acclaim that Amanda, in constant letters home, could hardly contain herself:

> *In The Huguenots . . . she comes on the scene mounted on a great elegant white horse, led by two grooms, and accompanied by two attendants on black horses. The music and scene of this*

opera surpass description!!! Every possible combination of scenic effect is brought to bear on this, the whole theatre is lighted with electric lights and the instrumentation of the imperial orchestra is grand beyond imagination and poor little Lilly Norton rides onto the scene with as much dignity and coolness as ever did the original—and the papers said she sang as no Queen could sing.

As ambitious as Amanda was for her daughter, the years away from New England weighed heavily on her heart. Edwin's health suffered, she had not yet met her grandchildren, and she was afraid she'd die without ever seeing Farmington again. But Lillie's desire to give her father a financially comfortable old age had borne fruit, and this was a comfort. The Imperial Opera was so pleased with La Nordica that they offered her $2,500 to sing for the following winter season. Always an astute businesswoman, Lillie held out for $4,000—and received it.

Later that first winter, terrible news arrived from Boston. Edwin had died on Christmas Eve. Both mother and daughter had hoped so keenly to return home that summer and share their success with Edwin, but now it was too late. They pressed on. Lillie sang in Europe and back in St. Petersburg for a second winter. Never content to rest, she signed on with the Paris Opera, realizing another of her ambitions. But this meant learning French and the French opera repertoire. Not only did Lillie become the prima donna of the Paris season, couturiers named a new color, as well as a new cloak, "La Nordica." At last Lillie and her mother were living a life of luxury. Opera stars of that era were treated like royalty; it was not unusual for admirers to give them diamonds and other expensive jewelry.

While in Paris that season of 1882, Lillian received a check for $10,000 and later a proposal of marriage from Frederick Allen Gower, a second cousin whom she'd met once many years before. Cousin Fred had grown into a handsome and important international businessman and reputed partner of Alexander Graham Bell. At Frederick's insistence, Lillie broke her contract with the Paris Opera for a forfeit of $10,000 so that they could be married in May of 1883. Frederick Gower was so wealthy, the money seemed a trivial matter. In September, Lillie, her new husband, and her mother sailed for home. After a wonderful family reunion and concert in Farmington, however, Lillie found herself without singing engagements.

Her New York City debut, on November 26, 1883, in *Faust*—billed as Lillian Norton Gower—received only lukewarm reviews. For her next performance, she returned to the name Nordica. Some of the Boston papers criticized her voice, but Lillie dazzled Chicago. The triumph was short-lived, however, when Frederick Gower—who'd been traveling on business—suddenly reappeared and whisked Lillie back to New York, supposedly angry that she'd received only second billing. Because of Frederick's insistence that Lillie break her contract with the Paris Opera, her career in France seemed over, and now her American tour had ended too.

Amanda had grown to despise her son-in-law, as it became more clear that he hated opera and didn't want his wife to sing at all—even at home. His violent outbursts terrified Lillie, and when he ordered Amanda out of his London house, Lillie went with her. Lillian's mental and physical health broke down. Back in Boston, she petitioned the courts for independent income on grounds of abuse, allegations Frederick planned to fight. But, in July of 1885, he disappeared on an experimental balloon flight across the English Channel and was never seen again. It turned out that he'd managed to squander his fortune as well.

Six months after she was widowed, Lillie returned to performing on a well-received American tour, and then she and her mother set sail for England. There, Lillie learned the English oratorio style and became the toast of London, singing with the world-famous tenor Jean de Reszke. While she enjoyed the life of a prima donna in London, she was never content unless pursuing a new dream: She'd long wanted to perform at the Bayreuth Festival in Germany, where Richard Wagner's operas were presented—and where no American had ever been invited to sing.

In 1891, while keeping up a rigorous schedule of operas and concerts in London, Lillie happened to sing with the young Hungarian baritone Zoltan Dome, who'd made a splash that season. They were attracted to each other, but she felt wary of marriage, and each had a career to nurture.

Amanda Norton, who'd soldiered on at her daughter's side year after year, far from home, finally died on November 28, 1891, a bitter loss for Lillie. Her London apartment felt empty without the constant companionship of her mother, best friend, wisest critic, and staunchest admirer. Having grown up in a big family, Lillie longed for a lively household, wished she had children, and missed her parents, sisters, nieces, and nephews, to whom she'd always felt close. But she had her singing, and it was her life.

In November of 1893, Lillie appeared as a regular member of the Metropolitan Opera in New York. Then Richard Wagner's widow, Cosima, a zealous protector of his work, invited her to appear at Bayreuth, Germany, in the summer of 1894, singing the role of Elsa in *Lohengrin*. Lillie knew the opera, but in Italian not German, and mastering Cosima's staging methods as well as the German language meant months of study. Still, Lillie was happy to achieve another of her dreams, and not just for her own sake: Zoltan Dome was hired to sing the role of Parsifal. Lillie's Elsa moved and delighted German audiences, including Cosima Wagner. Blinded—and apparently deafened—by love, however, Lillie imagined Dome's Parsifal was also wonderful, but few others shared that judgment, and his career at Bayreuth quickly ended. Nevertheless, Nordica and Dome were soon engaged, although Lillie seemed in no rush to marry—as if she were waiting for Zoltan to prove himself. In the meantime, she pursued her own career with zeal.

For all her level-headedness and discipline when it came to singing, Lillie was foolhardy in her romantic life. Suddenly, in the spring of 1896, Dome arrived in Indianapolis, where Lillie had been appearing, and insisted that they be married. During the seven years their marriage lasted, Zoltan Dome was vain and lazy, and a notorious philanderer. Finally, after one too many proofs of his infidelity, Lillian sued for divorce.

As the years passed and Lillian neared fifty, she knew that her singing days were numbered. Instead of reducing her concerts, however, she increased them with a triumphant tour of the United States. Not simply a legendary singer and renowned personality, she was now an institution. Her image—considered the height of American elegance and beauty—appeared in Coca-Cola advertising campaigns of the period. During the fall and winter of 1907, Lillie gave nearly sixty concerts in fifty cities and small towns. For all of them, she wore evening gowns designed by the House of Worth, draped herself in jewels, and sang beloved arias and songs.

In July of 1908, Nordica married for the third time, this time to a millionaire named George Washington Young, who'd sent her an emerald necklace after attending one of her concerts. The Youngs honeymooned in France, then sailed to New York, and Lillie again toured the country. During this trip she talked to many women dedicated to the suffrage movement, and she herself became an ardent suffragist. She also decided to wear only American-made gowns. Whenever she could, she spoke out in favor of women gaining the vote and earning equal pay for equal work.

In August of 1911, Lillie and George visited Farmington. For her birthday, her sisters had bought and repaired the little family farmhouse, a gift she greatly loved. She was happy to give a concert for free in her beloved hometown. On August 17, horses, buggies, and motorcars lined the streets of Farmington, and the auditorium filled long before the concert began. Ferns and goldenrod, picked from nearby fields, decorated the stage. The next day newspapers around the country trumpeted the event: "Familiar Old Songs Move Her Fellow Townspeople to Tears. . . . Weatherbeaten farmers and their wives sat in the audience and accorded the singer one of the most heartfelt tributes she has ever received."

George Young was an aggressive businessman, but early in their marriage, his affairs began to unravel and he lost vast amounts of money. Time and again, Lillie came to the rescue. Meanwhile, she was as busy as ever, but any illusions she had about George soon vanished. When she admitted, "I'm a poor picker of husbands," no one disagreed. Also at this time, the knowledge that her vocal powers would soon wane sometimes rose like a shadow, though her voice remained quite strong and expressive. To escape her unhappy home, as well as to challenge herself while she could still sing, Lillie organized a concert tour of Australia and New Zealand in the summer of 1913.

The schedule was demanding, and Lillie fell ill in Australia, but she managed to put on grand performances and decided to continue on to Java as she'd originally planned. The train from Sydney to Melbourne on December 17 was so late that she almost missed the *Tasman*'s sailing. But when her manager sent a telegram to the captain, he held the ship in port. Unfortunately, ten days later, the *Tasman* hit a coral reef and stuck there until another ship pulled it free. Lillie kept her courage, but before the ship could limp to the nearest port, hurricane winds and rains blasted it, and Lillie developed pneumonia. For three months she languished on remote Thursday Island, plagued by fevers. She recovered enough to sail for Batavia, but then, early on the morning of May 10, 1914, she whispered, "I am coming, Mother," and died. She was fifty-seven.

Although Lillie had just drafted a new will, few of her last wishes were honored, except her desire to be cremated. The money she wanted to share with her sisters was eaten up by legal expenses. La Nordica was one of the last great nineteenth-century opera divas, a star from the Golden Age, and people everywhere mourned her passing, but it seemed that she might be forgotten as World War I engulfed Europe and the United States.

But Farmington, Maine, would never forget Lillie Norton. In 1927, townspeople bought the farmhouse where she was born, renovated the property, and opened the Nordica Homestead Museum. Open every summer, the museum "displays many artifacts from her extraordinary career, including original gorgeous stage gowns and dazzling tiaras and jewelry, as well as her entire collection of opera scores." Nordica Auditorium graces the nearby campus of the University of Maine at Farmington. On March 17, 1943, the Yankee Diva received another honor: the USS *Lillian Nordica* was launched at South Portland, Maine, the first Liberty ship named for a musical artist. As recently as 2011, the Nordica Cinema opened its doors in Freeport, Maine. Lillie sings on.

Josephine Diebitsch Peary

(1863–1955)
Arctic Explorer and Writer

On the afternoon of September 6, 1909, the ink-blue waters of the Atlantic lapped at the rocky shores of Eagle Island in Casco Bay, Maine. As clouds drifted down the sky, they built, wave upon wave, into horses and trains and fields of candy snow. A "typical Maine day"—so beautiful, hard-won and precious.

The sun was strong enough to warm Josephine Peary's back as she bent to cut pink and white phlox for a bouquet, but the light had already tipped toward blue, signaling a change. In the garden crickets sang, *hurry, hurry; time is short*. There would be more fine, summerlike days before she, her sixteen-year-old daughter, Marie Ahnighito, and six-year-old son, Robert Jr., left the island for the winter, but a cool, bright wind, fresh from Canada, kept the temperatures in the sixties, a reminder of what was to come.

So many times that day, Josephine's thoughts flew north as they always did, beyond the wind, beyond Canada, to northernmost Greenland and the Arctic Circle. For twenty-three years, her husband, Robert E. Peary, had searched for the North Pole. She had accompanied him on three expeditions and met him several times in Greenland. A respected Arctic explorer in her own right, she was also a renowned writer and lecturer. But now she waited. It had been months since she'd heard from her husband. After so many failed attempts, had he reached the

Josephine Diebitsch Peary   The Maine Women Writers Collection, University of New
England, Portland

North Pole? Was he still alive? She knew the dangers. She'd lived them herself: blinding snowstorms, the disorientation of endless white and gray, crevasses that swallowed dogs and sledges, cold beyond any cold imaginable, nights that lasted half a year. You must get used to waiting, people assumed. You never get used to waiting, Josephine knew.

Holding the spicy-smelling phlox, Josephine rose to her feet. She couldn't let herself imagine disaster. Instead, she admired the bay gleaming like wet gold. Among the lobster boats and day sailers, she saw two motorboats heading toward the island from the direction of South Harpswell, on the far shore. She wasn't expecting visitors. Robert had bought Eagle Island in 1881, and theirs was its only house, built high on granite bluffs, like the pilothouse of a ship sailing northeasterly. For a moment, Josephine's heart beat faster. Maybe there was some word. But no, it couldn't be.

In a few moments, the first boat tied up at the island's mooring. A man scrambled into a skiff and rowed to shore, eager to deliver a telegram into Josephine's hand. She dropped the flowers and nervously ripped open the envelope. Inside was a message from the Associated Press: Peary has reached the Pole. The man could hardly contain himself, but Josephine didn't get overly excited. Too many false alarms had made her wary. Soon the second boat dropped anchor, and another man, red faced and sweating, ran up the lawn. It was Mr. Palmer, the storekeeper and postmaster of South Harpswell. He also carried a telegram, this one from Peary himself: "Have made it at last. . . ."

On April 6, 1909, he had planted the US flag at 90 degrees north latitude: the first man, he believed, to stand at the top of the world. It had taken him five more months to reach Indian Harbor, Labrador, from where he cabled his accomplishment.

Soon other newspapermen swarmed Eagle Island. Josephine could hardly believe it. All those years; now success. And Robert would be coming home soon, for good, she hoped. At last!

"What do you say now, Mrs. Peary?" one reporter asked.

A woman of great dignity but also high spirits, Josephine responded, "I say, come on, boys, let's have a drink."

Josephine, born in Washington, DC, on May 22, 1863, was the eldest daughter of wealthy and well-educated parents, Herman Henry Diebitsch of Prussia and Magdelena Augusta Schmid Diebitsch of Saxony. Herman taught languages at the Smithsonian Institution, a vibrant center for learning of all kinds. Jo, as she preferred to be called, had two younger brothers, Emil and Henry, and a younger sister, Marie, nicknamed Mayde. Hers was a loving, cultured family, one that encouraged her curiosity and independence. As a girl she was an avid reader. "I always revered learning and scientific investigation and intellectual victories," she would later write.

After graduating from public high school in Washington, she studied at a business college, then worked as a clerk in the exchange department of the Smithsonian. Pictures from the era show an elegantly dressed young woman with full lips, thick dark hair, and firm eyebrows highlighting a frank, steady gaze. A "belle of the capital" as W. H. Hobbs, a Robert Peary biographer, described her, Josephine was not only beautiful and adventurous, she also had a firm, practical bent and a strong will, qualities that would be tested again and again in future years.

In 1885, while attending dancing school, Jo met Robert Edwin Peary, a handsome, twenty-nine-year-old Navy civil engineer, who'd grown up in Portland, Maine, and graduated from Bowdoin College. For three years they courted, much of it by mail, while "Bert" organized a survey for a possible canal in Nicaragua, and, in 1887, traveled to Greenland for the first time. On August 11, 1888, when Jo was twenty-five, the two were married at the Diebitsches' stately Washington home. According to tradition, the groom selected the bride's bouquet, usually made of white flowers. But that afternoon, as the temperature hit 101 degrees, Jo carried—at her own insistence—a handful of red roses instead.

Jo and Bert lived in New York, then Philadelphia, where he worked on various naval civil engineering projects. But his northern adventure had sparked other dreams, which Josephine shared: to cross Greenland's ice cap and find the North Pole. The Pearys were not alone in their ambitions. By the 1870s, the United States had at least partially recovered from the devastation of the Civil War, and its focus shifted outward to explore—and dominate—unknown worlds. Now Americans joined Italians and Norwegians in search of the same prize: to claim for their own countries the exact spot, on a flowing sea of ice, where every direction is south: the geographic North Pole. The race was on.

Soon after their wedding, Robert Peary began actively organizing an expedition to reach the northern end of Greenland via the inland route. He found sponsorship from the American Geographical Society, the Brooklyn Institute, and the Philadelphia Academy of Sciences. Not only was Josephine central in planning for the trip, she also helped raise money. She wasn't shy about tapping her family's many connections at the Smithsonian and in Washington, DC, nor did she have any intention of waving to Robert's ship as it disappeared below the horizon.

In June of 1891, a party of seven explorers set sail from New York bound for Greenland on the steam-powered whaling barkentine *Kite*. Jo was among them, the first woman ever to take part in an Arctic expedition. Other members included Eivind Astrup, a Norwegian skier; Frederick A. Cook, a surgeon; and Matthew Henson, Peary's African-American valet. Newspapers, eagerly following the story, reported that Peary was "crazy" for bringing along a woman and a black man. Such attitudes helped forge a strong friendship between Jo and Henson, who would become perhaps the most highly skilled explorer on Peary's team.

Jo's resolve was tried early on when Peary broke his leg on shipboard. She nursed him and cooked for the whole group, as well as tended Redcliffe House, the two-room home they built on the shores of McCormick Bay, halfway between the Arctic Circle and the North Pole.

Within a few weeks—before ice locked it in place for the winter—the *Kite* sailed south, not to return for a year. The small party was alone now, dependent on each other for companionship and survival.

One day, while Robert was still recovering from his leg fracture, the group went by boat to hunt walruses. In their excitement they ran aground on an ice floe, where some 250 aggressive walruses attacked the boat. Jo crouched down to protect Robert's vulnerable leg with her own body; meanwhile, she calmly loaded the men's rifles as they fired shot after shot. Jo's calmness and hands-on courage that day won the men's admiration. She earned their devotion by preparing special feasts to celebrate each birthday and holiday, when, so far from home, spirits sagged.

During that year Jo grew to be a skilled hunter of reindeer, ptarmigan, and other game, which the party needed for clothing as well as for food. She tended her own trap lines, kept a sidearm, and was a fine shot with her Winchester rifle. She was interested in everything—wildflowers, glaciers, Inuit customs—and she kept scrupulous notes about the expedition, published in 1901 as the groundbreaking work, *My Arctic Journal: A Year Among Ice-Fields and Eskimos.*

At first Jo shared the common American prejudices of her era; she described the Inuits as "smelly," "odd" people, uncultured and uncouth. But soon her curiosity, friendliness, and sense of humor—and theirs—carried the day. She realized quickly that the expedition's only chance at success lay in adapting the Inuits' survival techniques. She learned their language and asked the women to teach her how to make Arctic clothing. Though she wouldn't chew the skins to soften them, as the Inuits did, she used their patterns, spending hours working with them to make bearskin pants, snowshoe hare stockings, waterproof sealskin boots, fur coats, and mittens of deerskin.

In 1893, pregnant with her first child, Jo again set sail with Robert on a larger expedition: the goal, to explore land north of Greenland, and again, if possible, reach the North Pole. Their base of operations that year was Anniversary House, a small building on Greenland's Bowdoin Bay. It was here, in September, that she delivered her daughter, Marie Ahnighito Peary, the first white child born that far north, at less than 13 degrees from the North Pole. The name "Ahnighito" honored the Inuit woman who made the baby's first fur suit. Marie was nicknamed "The Snow Baby" for her startling snow-colored skin and northerly birthplace.

During that winter, living in darkness except for the light of oil lamps, Jo fed her daughter and rocked her to sleep inside Anniversary House. Then in February, the sun finally rose over the mountains, flooding Bowdoin Bay with light. Jo placed Ahnighito in the middle of a bed heaped with furs. Here sunlight, shining through a high window, touched the baby's skin. Eagerly, she stretched out her fingers to meet the strange bright beams, "just as if she was bathing in perfumed golden water," Josephine wrote. "It was the first time she had ever seen the sun."

While Robert stayed on for another two years, Jo sailed home the following summer. Her parents, brothers, and sister had yet to meet Marie Ahnighito, who was already toddling and saying words. Robert returned home in 1896. A year later, Josephine and Marie Ahnighito returned with him to Bowdoin Bay. Jo recorded the events of Marie's first year and her visit to her birthplace in a very popular children's book, *The Snow Baby*, published in 1901. As she had done in *My Arctic Journal*, she was able to re-create the wonders and hardships of the northern world she was beginning to know well. *The Snow Baby* is full of information about Arctic landscape and animal life, as well as Inuit culture. It shows Jo's interest in science and human nature, and her lyrical eye for detail. In this passage, she describes summer's coming:

*The great sheet of snow-covered sea-ice over which the hunters
had driven their dogs and sledges was beginning to soften under*

the caresses of the summer sun. Pools of water began to collect like cool green shadows on the white rolling surface, while numerous black specks on the white sheet showed where sleeping seals were sunning themselves beside their front doors, which opened in the deep sea.

Separated by thousands of miles during much of their married life, Jo and Bert tried to keep in touch by letter. Often she would make five copies of a single letter and send them off on five different whaling ships, in hopes that one might reach her husband. For months, sometimes years, she had no idea if he were even alive.

In a letter dated March 1900, and written from their home on Twelfth Street NW, Washington, DC, Jo told Robert about the death of their second child, a tragedy she'd had to face alone. Here, in words meant only for him, we can glimpse the private toll their life exacted.

If only the time since last August has not been as hard for you as it has for me is all I ask & pray for mightily. . .

Surely we ought not both to suffer & I have suffered for both. Our little darling, whom you never knew was taken from me on Aug 7, '99 just 7 months after she came. She was only sick a few days but the disease took right hold of her little head & nothing could be done for her. . . . But oh my husband I wanted you, how much you will never know. I shall never feel quite the same again, part of me is in the little grave. The news of your terrible suffering came soon after. . . . It nearly prostrated me, but you know I am strong & can bear & bear & bear.

Soon after writing this letter, Jo organized her own expedition to help Peary recuperate from his "terrible suffering," the amputation of eight frostbitten toes. She and Marie Ahnighito were forced to over-winter three hundred miles south of Peary's camp, however, when their ship, the *Windward*, struck an iceberg en route. That same winter, Jo met Peary's pregnant Inuit lover, Allakasingwah. In spite of the pain this must have caused her, she remained supportive of his work in every possible way.

Once the Pearys' son, Robert Jr., was born in 1903, Josephine no longer traveled north. Robert grew increasingly obsessed and single-minded, and the weight of his failure to reach the Pole wore him down. Jo published articles about her own Arctic adventures, as well as his, and gave illustrated lectures to raise money, keeping his quest in the public eye. On September 6, 1909, when the telegram announcing his success arrived on Eagle Island, it was a shared victory, a family triumph.

Although Peary was the Charles Lindbergh of his day, incredibly famous and admired, he was also dogged by controversy. Another explorer, Dr. Frederick A. Cook, the surgeon who'd set Peary's leg in 1891, insisted that he had reached the North Pole first, in April of 1908. The controversy swept scientific circles and reached the general public, who first sided with Cook, until a group commissioned by the National Geographic Society agreed that Peary's claim was the more believable. (In the 1980s, new calculations indicated that probably neither Peary nor Cook had reached the geographic North Pole, but the issue remains unresolved.)

At last, once the Navy had granted Peary the status of rear admiral, and an admiral's retirement, he put Arctic exploration behind him. The family now spent summers on Eagle Island together. Robert became interested in aviation and the uses that planes might have in defending the country. After his death from pernicious anemia in 1920, Jo moved from Washington to Portland, Maine, for the winters. Summers she lived on Eagle Island with her children and grandchildren.

Reflecting on her life, Jo once told a reporter, "I have looked on the Frozen Deep as an old friend, as well as a vast phenomenon to be solved." The Peary family's connection with the Arctic was a profound and lasting one. Their daughter, Marie Ahnighito Peary Stafford, wrote books about the Arctic—several with her mother as coauthor—and promoted her father's accomplishments. Robert E. Peary Jr. was a civil engineer and an Arctic explorer as well. In 1955, the National Geographic Society awarded Josephine its highest honor, the Medal of Achievement. That same year, on December 19, she died at home—290 Baxter Boulevard, in Portland—at the age of ninety-two. She was buried next to her husband in Arlington National Cemetery.

Not long after her death, Jo's children donated Eagle Island to the State of Maine. During the summer, it's still open to the public, a beautiful rocky place with trails and wide vistas of ocean and sky. The house serves as a museum, full of family memorabilia and Arctic treasures from fur skins to narwhal tusks, from photographs to Inuit tools and clothing. Jo's presence still graces Eagle Island. Her own words, published over a hundred years ago in *My Arctic Journal*, evoke the extraordinary woman she was:

> *Two very old women in particular were led to me, and one of them, putting her face close to mine . . . scrutinized me carefully from head to foot, and then said slowly, "Uwanga sukinuts ammissuare, koona immartu ibly takoo nahme," which means, "I have lived a great many suns, but never have seen anything like you."*

FLORENCE NICOLAR SHAY

(1884–1960)

Penobscot Basketmaker and Tribal Advocate

Florence sat in the workroom adjoining her kitchen, weaving a basket of brown ash splints and sweetgrass. Nestled on her lap was the basket's base, which she'd shaped around a wooden mold, smoothed down by generations of use. She wove quickly and steadily. Hers were practiced hands. She was seventy-four, and she'd been making baskets since girlhood, a skill and an art—as well as a tool for economic survival—passed down from her mother and her mother's mother.

It was mid-January, 1958. While she worked, Florence listened to her favorite Saturday radio broadcast of classical music. A Chopin sonata was playing. Only 3:00 p.m. and already sunlight had turned to slanting gold. In just a week she and Leo would celebrate their fiftieth wedding anniversary. For a moment her fingers grew still as she gazed out the window at the Penobscot River, which surrounded Indian Island, part of the Penobscot reservation where she'd spent most of her life. Always the river beckoned—pathway, source of food and livelihood, spiritual heartbeat. It had been frozen since November, and on its white expanse, wind had sculpted snow into peaked waves and long blue shadows, stark and elegant as eagle wings. Upriver, beyond the mills of Old Town, the sun's oblique rays glittered through the geometry of bare tree branches. She picked up an ash splint, which she'd dyed herself, the

Florence Nicolar Shay Charles N. Shay and family

deep blue of predawn. Chopin's music danced. Gold sunlight touched her white hair, the blue splint.

Florence's calm industry belied another part of her makeup, not so apparent to someone watching her weave a basket that afternoon: her boldness on behalf of the Penobscot people. "This feisty lady had had the temerity to write to President Franklin Delano Roosevelt and complain that the State of Maine had taken away her right to vote," says historian Neil Rolde in his book *Unsettled Past, Unsettled Future: The Story of Maine Indians.* Florence, herself, in a fifteen-page booklet called *History of the Penobscot Tribe,* written and self-published in 1933, described the situation with characteristic clarity and honest fire:

> *In 1924, during President Coolidge's administration, an act was passed by Congress conferring citizenship upon all Indians born within the territorial limits of the United States. My husband and I and our family lived in Connecticut from 1923 to 1930. During the presidential election of 1928, we registered as citizens of the United States and voted as such with no questions asked as to our right. After we returned to Maine, we, with my sister, went to the registration board of Old Town, Maine, to register as citizens in our home town, but we were met with a distinct refusal, as an obsolete law of the State of Maine forbids the registration and voting by Indians, and in that law we are classed with criminals, paupers, and morons.*

After the United States entered World War II—and Maine Indians were still denied suffrage—Florence added this protest to the 1942 reissue of her booklet: "I have four sons and I feel the government has not the right to draft my boys without giving us the right to vote. . . . We are a segregated, alienated people and many of us are beginning to feel the weight of the heel that is crushing us to nothingness."

But Florence didn't simply write pamphlets and letters, then passively wait for a response. In spite of her personal reticence, she was an activist, following a long family tradition, lived out in her own unique way.

Florence Estelle Nicolar entered the world on August 5, 1884, at Indian Island, the youngest of three daughters born to Joseph and Elizabeth Josephs Nicolar. One sister, Emma, was already fourteen when Florence was born; Lucy was two. The girls' parents were a remarkable couple. Joseph came from an impressive line of Penobscots, among them John Neptune, a powerful chief elected lieutenant governor for life in 1816. Joseph himself was a very intelligent, educated man, who served more terms as tribal representative to the state legislature than any other Penobscot. In addition to land surveying, farming, hunting, and fishing, he wrote feature stories about Penobscot culture and history. In 1893, he wrote and published a book entitled *The Life and Traditions of the Red Man.*

Florence's mother, Elizabeth Nicolar, called Lizzie, was also a powerhouse. Twenty-one years younger than Joseph, she was smart, beautiful, and skilled not only at making baskets but at promoting their sales, a gifted leader and organizer. Florence and her sisters were raised in an intellectually ambitious and political family. This strong foundation bolstered them for the years they would spend advocating for educational, economic, and social justice for their tribe.

For thousands of years, the Penobscots had roamed freely over a vast territory in the Penobscot River watershed. No boundaries, no state lines, no reservations. With three other woodlands tribes in the Northeast—the Passamaquoddy, Mik'maq, and Maliseet—they formed the Wabanaki Confederation. The Wabanakis followed nature's rhythms. In the winter they lived in small settlements scattered throughout the region's forests. In late spring they canoed to the coast, escaping insects and enjoying summer's bounty of fish, shellfish, and berries.

In 1797, the Penobscot tribe deeded most of what is now Maine to Massachusetts—before the two became separate states. In return, their reservation consisted of 140 small islands in the Penobscot River between Old Town and Mattawamkeag, and they were to receive annual monetary and other subsidies. But these soon stopped: Treaty conditions were broken, promises betrayed.

During Florence's lifetime, the seasonal rhythm of her forebears remained, motivated now by economic necessity. The fall, winter, and spring months were spent on Indian Island, where she and her sisters attended the Catholic mission primary school. Lizzie taught them how to make baskets, and they organized sweetgrass braiding parties with other island women. The Nicolars' was a lively household, filled with music and laughter. Many Penobscots played musical instruments, so impromptu concerts were common, as well as lectures and other events held at the church. Florence loved playing the piano and practiced the hours it took to become an excellent musician.

In the summer, along with many other Penobscots from Indian Island, the Nicolars joined the seasonal migration to the Maine coast. With them on the train, they brought the baskets they'd made during the winter, as well as fresh supplies. Different families selected different resort communities. Florence's returned each year to Kennebunkport in southern Maine. There they set up a stand, selling baskets and making new ones. To attract more tourists, Lizzie encouraged Florence and Lucy to sing and dance. Dressed in traditional Indian outfits, they entertained potential customers. Lucy especially enjoyed this. Around the first of August, when their baskets sold out, the Nicolars returned to Indian Island.

In 1894, when Florence was only ten, her father died—a deep loss for the family and the tribe. Because Lizzie and the girls now had to support themselves, astute marketing of their baskets was essential. Soon, the three began taking part in sportsmen's exhibitions in Boston, New

York, and Baltimore. These extravaganzas featured displays of sporting gear and wilderness equipment. Maine's exhibit promoted not only sporting goods but a way of life: "rusticating," the kind of wilderness tourism for which the state was becoming famous. The encampment included a log cabin with stuffed moose and deer, Maine guides, and a small artificial lake. Noted sportswoman Cornelia "Fly Rod" Crosby was there, demonstrating fly-fishing, while nearby, the Nicolars made baskets and snowshoes. While Lizzie and her daughters played into white Americans' notions concerning the romantic exoticism of Indians (whom they lumped together into a single image of Plains-type western tribes), much to their credit, they did it with a clear-eyed sense of economic purpose and a desire to preserve their own distinct culture and traditions.

Florence was thirteen or fourteen when Lucy left for Boston to go to high school and study voice. Lucy then toured as "Princess Watahwaso" ("Bright Star"), singing, acting, and lecturing about Indian cultures, while Florence remained at home. Although the leap from Indian Island's mission primary school to public high school on the mainland often proved rocky for the few Penobscots who tried it, Florence adapted well and in 1906, at the age of twenty-two, she graduated from Old Town High. Still eager for education, she attended Shaw Business College in Bangor, twelve miles away. She was a quick study at the skills needed for secretarial work, one of few professions open to any woman at the time, let alone a Penobscot.

On January 25, 1908, Florence married Leo Shay. He was a bright and industrious fellow, also from Indian Island, and six years her junior. While living on the island, they had seven children: Winter, born in approximately 1909 (who died of appendicitis at sixteen); Hattie, born in 1910 or 1911; Lawrence William, called Billy, in 1912; Martha Doris, known as Madeline or Maddy, in 1916; Lucille, a few years later; and Thomas Leo in 1921. Another daughter died in infancy.

In spite of the couple's hard work, it was almost impossible to make a living on Indian Island or in nearby Old Town. Jobs were scarce; prejudice against hiring native people further shrank their prospects. Therefore, in 1923, the year her mother died, Florence moved with Leo to Connecticut. Florence was adamant that her children grow up with economic and educational chances unavailable on the reservation. Part of being a Penobscot mother in that era, she believed, meant training her offspring to compete in the white world, as her own mother had taught her to survive by making baskets. The Shay children were raised speaking English, the language of opportunity, another way in which Florence prepared them to be self-sufficient.

In Connecticut, Florence had two more sons: Charles Norman in June of 1924 and Patrick Joseph in May of 1926. While raising a family, she did office work at Chief Two Moons Laboratory in Waterbury. Chief Two Moons, a Lakota Sioux shaman, ran a successful business selling herbal remedies in drugstores and by mail order. When the Great Depression hit, however, jobs dried up, so Florence and her family returned to Indian Island. They moved into the two-story house where she'd grown up. Her sister Lucy also came back home with her future third husband, "Chief" Bruce Poolaw, a Kiowa and fellow entertainer, twenty-one years younger than she, with whom she'd been traveling on the vaudeville circuit. Lucy had a house built on the riverbank, facing Old Town. A decade or so later, she and Bruce created a two-story teepee gift shop next-door.

Times were tough on the island. Grinding poverty caused many hardships, and there were few chances for either a living wage or a sound education—troubles compounded by the island's isolation and the Penobscots' status as second-class citizens. Joining her sisters, Lucy and Emma, and her sister-in-law, Pauline Shay, Florence set out to help. They resuscitated the Indian Woman's Club, of which their mother had been a founder thirty-five years earlier. Its purpose: to promote

"Indian welfare, education and social progress." Soon they were again affiliated with the Maine Federation of Women's Clubs, as well as with the National Federation.

The first issue the women tackled was the right to educational opportunity. Not satisfied with the quality of the Indian Island school for her own family, Florence wanted all Penobscot children to have the option to attend Old Town's public schools. In 1931, the Maine legislature passed such a bill into law. But it came at a price. The women were "expelled" from the island's Catholic church for challenging the status quo. Finally, after a difficult struggle, a group of Penobscots, including Florence, was able to establish a Baptist church on the island.

Each summer, starting in the early 1930s, Florence brought her baskets to the Maine coast, as she'd done in childhood. She and Leo set up a tent store, the Indian Camp Basket Shop, on Route 1 in Lincolnville Beach, between Belfast and Camden on Penobscot Bay. Helped by Leo and the children, she spent her days weaving baskets and selling them to tourists, a mainstay of the family's income. Florence's son, Billy Shay, eventually carried on the family tradition. Caron Shay, Billy's daughter, a master basketmaker like her father and grandmother, observes that Florence's baskets were beautiful to look at and beautifully made, "known for their symmetry, fine craftsmanship, and lasting quality." She also created her own dyes, now a vanishing art.

As busy as Florence was raising a large family and weaving baskets, she made time to advocate for two other longtime dreams, besides better education: Indian suffrage and a bridge connecting Indian Island to the mainland. For generations, Penobscots had traveled back and forth to Old Town in a fourteen-passenger rowboat. The fare was two cents each way. With its brick and frame buildings, its church spires and smokestacks, Old Town was home to paper and textile mills. Each winter Penobscots would spread a thick trail of sawdust on the ice so they could travel back and forth to work, attend school, and buy supplies.

Sometimes the trip was perilous: in spring, before ice-out when thin spots broke through; in late fall, when a sudden thaw eroded yesterday's solid track. There were accidents, drownings. During other seasons, when storms raged, the little ferry wouldn't run at all. Because of these physical dangers, added to the psychological isolation they created for Indian Island residents, Florence worked to make sure a connecting bridge was built.

For decades, the sisters spoke before the Maine legislature, organized committees, wrote letters, and circulated petitions. It would take until November 29, 1950—when Maine's governor officially dedicated the new bridge—for this part of their dream to become a concrete and steel embodiment of opportunity, but they endured as a family alliance, undaunted by setbacks and naysayers.

In her fascinating chapter about Lucy Nicolar, published in the collection *Of Place & Gender: Women in Maine History*, anthropologist Bunny McBride contrasts the different strengths Lucy and Florence brought to their shared endeavors, seeing Lucy's extroverted style as a complement to Florence's more self-contained reserve. She notes that Florence "was a quiet but firm presence, a careful thinker more likely to voice her views with pen than tongue. Lucy referred to her as the 'tribal scholar.'" Another of Florence's granddaughters, Emma Nicolar, describes Florence, Lucy, and Emma as "all dynamic women, married to very active and dynamic men." Florence's husband, Leo Shay, nicknamed "the manager," served two terms as the Penobscots' representative to the Maine legislature.

When the United States entered World War II, Florence and Leo joined the war effort at Boston's Charlestown Naval Shipyard. She worked in the office and he built boats. Their four sons were drafted—although they still did not have the right to vote. Charles, the second to the youngest, served as a combat medic. He landed on Omaha Beach and crossed the Rhine into Germany, where he was taken prisoner of war. While Florence was very patriotic and felt proud of her family's sacrifices, the political irony was not lost on her.

In the fall of 1945, when Charles came home on furlough, the family took the ferry to Old Town and again tried to vote in a small local election. It must have been an impressive sight: Florence and Leo, Pauline, Lucy and Bruce, joined by other family members. At the head of the line stood Charles Norman Shay: highly decorated combat veteran and former POW, in his dress uniform, studded with medals. Yet they were turned away. "Idiots don't have any right to vote in this state," election workers told them. Eight years later, however, in 1953, they finally won: Maine's Indians gained the right to vote without changing their tax status. "They were so happy and proud of themselves the day they voted in Old Town," recalls Florence's granddaughter Emma Nicolar.

Emma fondly remembers her grandmother for more than her political activism. Food was scarce, but Florence cooked huge dinners for her extended family. Everyone was welcome, including Emma, who often showed up at mealtime. Florence loved good china and set the table with nice cloths and glassware. She modeled gracious living for her granddaughter, as well as the hard work and motivation to earn everything she had. Well into her seventies, Florence was healthy and vigorous; she made baskets, played the piano, helped her family, and remained active on behalf of her Penobscot community. On May 24, 1960, she and Leo were setting up for the summer season at their basket shop in Lincolnville Beach when she suddenly suffered a lung embolism and died. She was seventy-six.

Born into a dynamic family, Florence Nicolar Shay adapted the lessons of her parents, creating a life rich in personal artistic expression as well as practical and hard-won educational, social, and political advancements for her people. Her son Charles, who married an Austrian woman and lived and worked in Europe for forty years, returned each summer to Indian Island. He now lives in the house his Aunt Lucy built, and he opens her teepee shop in the summer. In the teepee, which he renovated extensively, are heirloom baskets his mother made. In his house are fine objects she collected, music she listened to and taught him to love. "She was revered by her children, grandchildren, and great-grandchildren," he says.

Granddaughter Emma shakes her head in admiration when she thinks about her grandmother and her Aunt Lucy. Knowing what few resources the women had on Indian Island, she marvels at how they found the time and the nerve to accomplish all that they did. "They were radicals," she says, "smart enough and courageous enough to leave a history." Thoughtful by temperament, strong by nature, deeply principled, and proud of her heritage, Florence dared to demand rights for the Penobscot people. While she lived to see many improvements, she believed there remained much still to do. Quiet Florence was the driving force in her family, recalls Emma. "When she spoke, you listened because you knew whatever she said was very important."

MARGUERITE THOMPSON ZORACH

(1887-1968)

*Avant-Garde Painter
of Robinhood Cove*

On her first day in Paris, twenty-one-year-old Marguerite Thompson attended an exhibition of paintings called the Salon d'Automne. It was a life-changing experience. Her very presence on the streets of Paris that fall of 1908 seemed unlikely, almost a miracle. Marguerite had grown up in Fresno, California, a dusty town in the San Joaquin Valley. A bright student as well as a talented artist, Marguerite had planned to study at Stanford University—her trunks had already been shipped—when her aunt, Harriet Adelaide Harris, sent her the money to come visit her in Paris. "Aunt Addie" was a retired teacher and a painter herself, who had lived in Paris since 1900. She not only looked forward to her niece's company but also hoped to expose her to European art and culture. Marguerite grabbed the chance.

It was a long, exhausting trip by train and steamship, but now, having just arrived in Paris and eager not to waste a moment, Marguerite entered the imposing Grand Palais on the Champs Elysées. Inside were over two thousand pieces of art by some six hundred forty artists. Marguerite was awestruck. The Salon d'Automne, established in 1903 as an alternative to the official salon, exhibited works by artists dubbed "The Fauves." At the Salon d'Automne of 1905, a well-known art critic had, in disgust, called the artists "fauves"—wild beasts—and the name

Marguerite Zorach in her studio, 1913 Zorach Studio Collection

had stuck. These avant-garde artists—Henri Matisse, André Derain, and Maurice Vlaminck, among others—used dazzling colors, squeezed directly from the tube, and applied them with bold brushstrokes. Colors clashed and canvases swirled with intense emotion. Instead of trying to capture the illusion of a three-dimensional world on a flat plane, the paintings highlighted their two-dimensional surface, as if calling out to the observer, "Look, I'm paint on canvas!"

Many visitors to the Salon d'Automne were shocked, even scandalized. But Marguerite gloried in what she saw. Something new was in the air—the thrill and the challenge of modernism. These paintings, particularly Matisse's, stirred her independent nature and questioning mind. In a career spanning sixty years, she would bring to life amazing artworks—from paintings to tapestries, from batiks to embroidered clothes and hand-hooked rugs—all of which evoked what Jessica Nicoll, director of the Smith College Museum of Art, calls "her truly modern spirit."

Marguerite Thompson, the daughter of Winifred Harris and William Thompson, was born in Santa Rosa, California, on September 25, 1887. Her mother was descended from New England seafarers. Her father, raised a Quaker in Pennsylvania, became a well-known lawyer for the Napa vineyards near Fresno, still a pioneer town when the family moved there in the early 1890s. Marguerite's was a refined upbringing. In addition to attending public school, she and her younger sister Edith were tutored at home in French, German, and piano.

Life for Marguerite revolved around art. From an early age, drawing absorbed her time, and she filled many notebooks with her drawings and sketches. She also loved the natural world, especially camping with her family at Yosemite and in the Sierra Nevada. After graduating from Fresno High School, she took postgraduate classes for a year then taught at a rural schoolhouse near Fresno. She was enrolled at Stanford in the fall of 1908 when her aunt's telegram arrived, inviting her to Paris.

Aunt Addie had traditional art training in mind, no doubt, but Marguerite was drawn to more avant-garde work. After failing the entrance exams for the École des Beaux-Arts (she'd never sketched a nude from life), she took lessons at various places until she found the Académie de La Palette. Here she studied with a progressive Scottish artist, John Duncan Fergusson. Soon after her arrival in Paris, Marguerite visited the American writer Gertrude Stein, who'd gone to Christian Science Sunday school in San Francisco with her aunt. Although she didn't attend Gertrude's salon often, she did meet Pablo Picasso there, whose cubist work would influence her own.

During the next three years studying in Paris and traveling through Europe, Marguerite soaked up new ideas and experimented with color and shape as she explored what kind of artist she would become. She exhibited at the Salon d'Automne of 1911, where her paintings used the vivid colors and forceful outlines of fauvism. She befriended a young English artist, Jessica Dismorr, with whom she studied, shared a studio, and traveled.

In March of 1911, a fateful event took place at a morning painting class at La Palette—Marguerite met fellow student William Finkelstein, who would become her husband and lifelong creative partner. William's family had emigrated from Lithuania when he was a boy and eventually settled in Cleveland, Ohio. He'd left school after eighth grade to apprentice with a lithographer and later attended night classes at the Cleveland School of Art. After several years studying art in New York, he finally went to Paris in 1910.

William, two years Marguerite's junior and new to the Paris avant-garde, was impressed by her talent and bemused by her modernist thinking. In his autobiography, *Art Is My Life*, he described watching her paint "a pink and yellow nude with a bold blue outline." When he'd asked if she knew what she was doing, she made it clear "she knew—and that was the beginning. But," he added, "I just couldn't understand why such a nice girl would paint such wild pictures." Marguerite "didn't look just like everyone else or dress like everyone else," he noted. "Even then she made her own clothes. She wore a black silk turban on the back of her head with an enormous red rose in the center—a fascinating hat. . . . She was shy but sure of herself and gave the impression of character."

For her part, Marguerite considered William "quite tied down by things and ideas," someone who might become "a very good painter of the kind that just misses being an artist." Marguerite was William's guide to this new art revolution, free from the rules of the past. It was Marguerite who urged him to "be just as artistic as you have it in you to be." Over the next months the two friends fell in love.

On October 5, 1911, Marguerite left Paris with Aunt Addie for extended travels through Egypt, Palestine, India, Korea, China, and Japan, before arriving back in California in April of 1912. Struck by the natural beauty of the places she visited, she made sketches and painted landscapes. She also wrote frequent letters to William, detailing what she saw, as well as her thoughts about art and the life they wished to share. To make a little money, she published a series of travel articles in the *Fresno Morning Republican* and was known to write fine poetry as well as prose. Her seven months in Asia and the Middle East exposed her to new cultures, geographies, and styles of art, which affected her artwork profoundly.

Back in Fresno, Marguerite struggled with the constraints of middle-class family life. Her parents hated her modernist paintings and tried to lure her back into the conventional world of society parties and teas. But she longed for the creative freedom of Paris, and she missed William. In October and November of 1912, she held her first one-woman show in Los Angeles, followed by a December show in her hometown. But Fresno could not hold her.

On December 24, 1912, Marguerite arrived in New York. William met her train and they were married that same day. They decided to take a new last name together and chose "Zorach," William's original given name, changed to William by a teacher in Cleveland. Now, as Marguerite and William Zorach, they settled in Greenwich Village. In an artistic explosion, Marguerite painted colorful canvases as well as original designs on yards and yards of unbleached muslin to decorate their apartment.

Two months after their marriage, the Zorachs exhibited paintings in the Armory Show of 1913, which art historian Roberta Tarbell refers to as "a landmark in the history of the development of early modern art in the United States." William's work received no mention in the press, but Marguerite's use of color left one newspaper critic appalled: "The pale yellow eyes and the purple lips of her subject indicate that the digestive organs are not functioning properly. I would advise salicylate of quinine in small doses."

Although some members of the public misunderstood and even ridiculed her work, Marguerite seemed unaffected. She was brave and clear about who she was and what she believed. She also had William's full support, and they continued to paint in the same studio, helping each other with canvases, with ideas, with promoting their paintings. Although they struggled financially, these were rich, exciting years, and their collaboration nurtured them both. They exhibited paintings in their studio as well as at galleries, and they were at the center of the avant-garde community of American artists in New York.

In 1913 the Zorachs moved to another apartment, on Washington Square, where they lived for almost twenty-five years. At Marguerite's insistence, however—regardless of how poor they were—they spent every summer "in nature," borrowing friends' homes in New York and New Hampshire. In March of 1915, Marguerite gave birth to their first child, a son named Tessim. In 1916, she was one of only seventeen artists selected to show work in the Forum Exhibition, another groundbreaking artistic event. Her paintings incorporated cubist fragmenting of objects as well as the bold colors of fauvism. The Zorachs spent that summer, and two others, in Provincetown, Massachusetts, where they designed and painted scenery for the Provincetown Players. In November of 1917, Dahlov, a daughter, was born in Windsor, Vermont.

After the birth of her children, Marguerite no longer had long stretches of uninterrupted time. While she never gave up painting, she did less of it than before. Instead, she turned her artistic energies to designing and making embroidered tapestries—she called them "tapestry paintings"—which engrossed her for the next twenty years. She delighted in the wonderful colors available in wool yarns, more intense and varied than those of oil paints. Using innovative modernist styles, she elevated traditional handicrafts to the level of fine arts. Of her tapestries she wrote:

> *They are like symphonies that move and develop and change and contain a lifetime of growth, of power, and tenderness; of sharp contrasts and delicate nuance. They are creations that satisfy the artistic desire. And there is physical work, that same fascination that keeps a sculptor chipping away stone until the form stands revealed.*

In 1919, the Zorachs spent the summer in Stonington, Maine, where William helped Marguerite create an embroidered panel, *Maine Islands*. Here began their lasting connection to Maine. The years 1919–20 marked a difficult time for Marguerite, however. While visiting William's family in Cleveland that fall, she caught influenza and was hospitalized for two months. In April, the Zorachs arrived in California to visit Marguerite's family. They stayed almost a year. Much of that time Marguerite was convalescing and unable to work.

In 1923, the Zorachs bought a tumbledown saltwater farm, built in 1820, on Robinhood Cove in Georgetown, Maine. It cost $2,000, which was given to them by family friends. Although winters were spent in Greenwich Village, this was Marguerite's true home. Often she would arrive in late April, before her husband finished teaching at the Art Students League or her children's school year ended. She designed, planted, and tended beautiful flower and vegetable gardens. The Zorachs both taught at the Skowhegan School of Painting for a few weeks each summer. The family kept a cow and horses and hayed their own fields. They raised Dalmatians. Three or four art students, who studied with William, lived at Robinhood Cove. It was a full and busy life with many visitors and much outdoor work to do. Often in the fall, when William and the children returned to New York, Marguerite stayed behind until late October to paint and to put the house and gardens to bed.

Because the Zorachs believed that children were born with an innate desire to learn, which most education discouraged, they enrolled Tessim and Dahlov in New York's first progressive school, the City and Country School, which Marguerite described to her friend Jessica Dismorr as "more free and modern than any I know of."

In addition to her artistic gifts, Marguerite possessed great practicality. Whereas William was a dreamer, she was levelheaded and a skilled domestic manager. Family members say she could do anything she set her mind to—from haying fields and milking cows to fixing broken furniture and managing family finances. At times Marguerite seemed aloof, remote from even those closest to her, but, notes Tessim's widow, Peggy Zorach, it wasn't an aloofness born of disdain. She just seemed preoccupied with her own inner world. "Marguerite had a real twinkle," Peggy adds, "and a delightful sense of humor."

For Marguerite, daily life offered endless potential for creative expression, whether or not it took place at an easel. Her daughter Dahlov remembers a home more vibrant and interesting than any of her friends':

Our walls were canary yellow; Adam and Eve were painted on one wall, with the snake winding down the tree. The floors were bright vermilion, and covered with rugs that my mother designed and hooked herself. She created large batik hangings and bed-spreads, and every piece of furniture was decorated, each chair rung a different color.

Some critics have commented that Marguerite's art career, a flaming comet in the teens and twenties—parallel to or even surpassing her husband's—was somehow diminished by domestic obligations, children to care for, homes to run. It's true that after William turned to sculpture in the 1920s, his fame did overshadow hers, but Dahlov insists that her mother never stopped painting or developing as an artist. No matter how shaky the family finances, they always seemed to have hired help, so that both Zorachs could work much of the day. "Whatever you put your hand to is a work of art," Marguerite believed. Her artistic energies were more diffusely directed than her husband's, and her work blurred the lines between fine arts and fine handicrafts. For many years the art world did not value her work as highly as it did William's.

There was also the question of temperament. More self-contained than her husband, Marguerite took what came her way; she didn't promote herself to the extent he did. "Father used to nag her to do more, to complete works," Tessim told interviewer Cynthia Bourgeault for a 1987 article in *Down East* magazine. "He always had faith that she was a gifted artist. But she couldn't be bothered with short deadlines and the politics of the art world."

In spite of her independent spirit, it must have been difficult at times for Marguerite to deal with the discrimination that women artists routinely faced. The Downtown Gallery in New York, which had exhibited the work of both Zorachs starting in 1927 or 1928, continued to show William until his death in 1966 but dropped Marguerite in 1934—a bitter blow. Marguerite was active in New York art circles and, as president of the New York Society of Women Artists, advocated tirelessly for greater access to exhibitions.

During the 1930s and early 1940s, Marguerite did a number of large tapestry commissions. Her work sold well and was in high demand. After finishing a nine-by-six-foot embroidered portrait of the Rockefeller family, she moved away from handwork. Her eyes may have started to bother her; also, she now had longer uninterrupted stretches of private time to devote to her work. In any case, during the last thirty years of her life, she returned to painting as her primary artistic pursuit. She often painted brightly colored landscapes from her travels, but most of them explored her adopted home, Maine. These were glory years as her own unique style flowered. Museum director Jessica Nicoll puts it this way:

> *With paintings like "Sunrise Robinhood Cove" (circa 1951), she seems to recapture the spiritual power and intuitive color sense of her canvases from 40 years before, but with the experience of having been a painter throughout those intervening years. We sense her thrill of the extraordinary beauty of reflections in the half-light of daybreak, especially the red-hot ball of sun as it ascends over the horizon to initiate a brilliantly-lit new day.*

Although their artwork took them in different directions, Marguerite and William continued their creative collaboration until William's death of congestive heart failure in Bath, Maine, in November of 1966. In her seventies, Marguerite suffered a series of minor strokes, but she remained productive until the last year of her life. She died in New York on June 27, 1968, at the age of eighty-one.

Today, Marguerite is highly regarded not only for her modernist paintings but for her extraordinary textiles. In the last several decades, the art world has taken renewed interest in her work, thanks in great part to the dedication of the Zorach family—daughter Dahlov Ipcar (a Maine artist herself), son Tessim Zorach, and his wife Peggy. Though Tessim and Dahlov's husband, Adolph, have died in recent years, Dahlov still lives on Robinhood Cove. Until recently when Peggy moved into an assisted living facility, the two were neighbors, in adjacent old white farmhouses filled with vibrant paintings, rugs, and sculptures created over a lifetime. Marguerite and William's five grandsons have taken up the Zorach legacy as well.

For a young girl born to a proper nineteenth-century family, Marguerite's was a remarkable journey—from Fresno to Paris, from New York to Maine. Dahlov once described her as "independent and outspoken, a feminist ahead of her time. She was anti-establishment, anti-religious, pro-art, pro-creative." Her spirit was unique, her gifts truly modern. Nearly fifty years after her death, Marguerite remains an inspiration, full of creative fire, true to her own vision of what an artist's life well-lived might look like.

TOY LEN GOON

———◦●◦———

(1891–1993)

America's Mother of the Year, 1952

According to the Chinese lunar calendar, Toy Len Chin was born in the eighth month, fourteenth day (September 21) of 1891. Her birthplace, a mud brick hut, lacked running water and plumbing. Toy Len must have arrived without much fanfare—another daughter, the fifth of an eventual six children. Her parents, Chin Wah Feun and Eng Leong Ho, were tenant farmers in the village of old Gan Cun in Taishan City, a green, rainy place in Guangdong Province bordering the South China Sea. On the small parcel of land they rented, they grew rice in paddies, kept pigs, and raised taro and squash, as well as other vegetables. The whole family labored—the parents, three sons, and three daughters. Although Toy Len was intelligent and curious, schooling was out of the question. Rural peasant families such as hers rarely could afford the tuition, and even if there had been money, educating boys would have taken precedence over educating girls.

One of Toy Len's earliest daily chores was carrying water home from a nearby lake. Who could imagine, then, as she staggered under the weight of two full buckets balanced on a shoulder pole, that more than fifty years later and eight thousand miles from her childhood village, she'd be greeted at the White House in Washington, DC, by First Lady Bess Truman before a lunch honoring her as America's Mother of the Year?

Toy Len Goon, 1952 Courtesy of the family of Toy Len Goon

No one could, least of all Toy Len herself. She grew up in a Confucian world, animated by ghosts and spirits, a world of ancestor worship and strict deference to authority. Once, returning from the lake, she passed an elderly neighbor, whom she greeted respectfully but who did not answer in return. Her mother blanched when she heard this: That neighbor had died some weeks before. Another time, as Toy Len neared the lake, she heard loud splashing, which sounded like bird wings. But at the shoreline, she saw nothing—no birds, no ripples. It must be lake spirits playing, she decided.

Behind her on the path trotted one of the family's pigs. It was her favorite and followed her everywhere—to the paddies, to the garden, to the threshing floor. Other children teased Toy Len about her pet. But it didn't bother her. Soon enough the pig was slaughtered, its meat sold except for a meager portion kept for the Chins' supper. Even ninety-some years later, Toy Len remembered that long-ago pig and her own silent resistance to its fate. "I couldn't eat it," she told her daughter Doris.

She remembered the town crier, too, who walked the dirt lanes of Gan Cun each night, calling out reminders of proper behavior: "Wife, obey your husband. Husband, be good to your wife. Children, obey your parents." Even as a little girl, she seemed to accept life's hardships—the bone-weariness of farming, the attacks by bandits, the threat of starvation—and to understand the sacrifices and discipline needed to survive. And yet inside her there also existed, from the beginning, the bright flinty spark of who she was.

Although Toy Len probably never pictured herself living in America, she must have heard fantastic stories about Gum Shan, "Gold Mountain," to which thousands of young male Chinese peasants had flocked once word of the California gold rush reached them in 1849. At first these immigrants were welcomed. For a pittance, they helped prospectors pan for gold and dig into rock with pickaxes. In addition, they willingly performed jobs white forty-niners associated with women—cooking, cleaning, washing clothes. After gold rush fever died down, many Chinese immigrants joined work gangs responsible for the completion in 1869 of the Transcontinental Railroad connecting Missouri to San Francisco.

In the 1870s, the US economy slowed, and laborers competed for a shrinking number of jobs. Once encouraged to immigrate, the Chinese were now vilified—denied jobs and housing, subjected to acts of racist violence. Anti-Chinese propaganda filled the newspapers. In 1882, nine years before Toy Len was born, President Chester A. Arthur signed the Chinese Exclusion Act. It was the first such federal law directed at a particular ethnic group, and it meant that legal immigration from China stopped. Those Chinese already in America were not allowed to vote, own property, testify in court, marry non-Chinese, or bring their families from China. The growth of existing Chinatowns in cities such as San Francisco, New York, and Boston came to a standstill. Still, although immigration from China was illegal, peasants continued to enter the United States clandestinely rather than struggle in villages such as Gan Cun, Toy Len's childhood home.

Like those who left Gan Cun, Toy Len's family increasingly felt the terrible squeeze of poverty. When it finally seemed impossible to provide for six children, Toy Len's mother found a situation for her with a well-off merchant family, also named Chin. Toy Len was only ten. As a foster daughter, she did domestic chores and tended a new baby, calling the elders the familial "uncle" and "aunt." She always felt grateful for this life-saving chance.

At the age of about twelve, Toy Len began to spend any extra time she had at a "girls' house," as was the custom in Guangdong. Here, supervised by older women, she and her age-mates learned how to be wives, how to sew, how to groom themselves—including the shaping of eyebrows using thread—how to handle mothers-in-law, how to mourn, how to perform elaborate funeral rites. Here too, in safe female-only spaces, they memorized mournful songs about the cruel lot of women's lives. They also created close friendships, laughing and sharing secrets as they prepared for marriage and motherhood.

Toy Len worked hard and got along well with the members of her second family. She was so kind and good-natured that the matron of the household would have liked to adopt her and find her a husband. But before placing her daughter with the Chins, Toy Len's mother had already arranged her marriage to a Mr. Moy from the nearby village of Qi Bang. He came from a non-farming family, which was an important criterion for Eng Leong Ho. Her own family survived by farming, and she was insistent that her three daughters not endure that same exhausting life.

When Mr. Moy returned from America in 1911, he and Toy Len married. Because her own parents couldn't afford a dowry, matron Chin gave Toy Len bridal outfits worthy of her own daughter. She continued to treat Toy Len as family, making the traditional post-bridal visits to her new home a month later and including her in seasonal holidays. In her long, eventful life, Toy Len never forgot these acts of generosity. From the Chins, she later said, she had learned "how not to be petty."

Four months after the wedding, Moy sailed back to the United States while Toy Len stayed behind at her mother-in-law's house. (It seems the father-in-law had died.) Moy sent enough money home to support both women well, but only five years later, he died of tuberculosis in America. At only twenty-six, Toy Len was a widow. As soon as her mother heard about Moy's death, she went to a fortune-teller for guidance. The prediction: Toy Len would have bitterness and a hard life until age sixty.

Shaken by this information, Eng Leong Ho counseled her daughter to leave the Moy household. "They don't own property," she said. "There's no land to live off and no hope for the future. I need to find you a new prospect." But Toy Len had such a good relationship with her mother-in-law that she didn't want to leave. Her mother's response was swift and harsh. "I won't ever speak to you again unless you follow my command," she threatened. With great reluctance, Toy Len relented.

But finding another husband for a young widow was not an easy task. Nevertheless, Eng Leong Ho set to work. From a neighbor, she learned of a widow in the nearby village of Tong Tow who might be looking for a bride for her son. Widow Goon, fifty-four years old and in poor health, had had a daughter, Thlen Ho, and two sons. One, Doo Wong, died in childhood. To continue his lineage, widow Goon had adopted a boy, Doo Ngui. The second son, marriage-eligible Doo Gen (Dogan), was in America. Toy Len's mother immediately went to Tong Tow to explore the Goon family's financial and marriage situation. During the interview, the widow Goon bragged, "We're not a farming family." This was true, but just barely.

Widow Goon's husband had died when she was twenty-nine, leaving her a self-proclaimed "Merry Widow." Over the years she had sold off her husband's land piece by piece to support herself. Now she was down to the last parcel, which sharecroppers paid six bushels of grain a year to rent. To make matters worse, some years earlier her son Dogan had married a young woman who gave birth to a girl, Hung Gee, and then promptly ran off, leaving the baby with her mother-in-law. For the past seven years, widow Goon, by herself, had tried to raise both her adopted son Doo Ngui and Hung Gee, her granddaughter, now ages seven and eleven. Not surprisingly, what she prized most highly in a prospective bride for Dogan was her child-care ability.

Toy Len was well-qualified, and the widow Goon agreed to the match. It would be Toy Len's second arranged marriage. Once again, she accepted what life brought with courage and a resilient spirit. It was 1919 when she walked to Tong Tow from the Moy village. With the blessings of both mothers, Toy Len and Dogan were married by proxy; they had never met. During the wedding, she bowed and swore allegiance to her ancestors at the family altar while a rooster stood on a chair next to her, the traditional stand-in for a faraway groom. While Toy Len waited for Dogan to come for her, she took care of the children, nursed her mother-in-law, and managed the household.

Quarters there were tight. The three generations shared a house with Dogan's uncle's widow. Because the two elder women did not get along, a large piece of furniture was positioned to divide the small space in half. Toy Len, however, managed to stay on good terms with both her mother-in-law and her aunt-by-marriage.

Dogan himself had emigrated to America around 1912 at the age of nineteen. Because of the Chinese Exclusion Act, he had entered the United States illegally. Using family connections on the East Coast, he found jobs at hand laundries and restaurants in Chinatowns in New York and Boston. After brief stints in Lawrence and Lowell, Massachusetts, he moved to Portland, Maine, where he was hired at a laundry.

In mid-August 1917, three months after the United States entered World War I, Chinese Inspector John McCabe of Boston arrested Dogan at the laundry and took him to jail. "Hold Chinaman for Illegal Residence" read the headline in the *Portland Evening Express* that day. Dogan had to pay $1,500 in bail to be released. At his deportation hearing that fall, he claimed he was, in fact, a US citizen, born in San Francisco of legal Chinese immigrants. A Chinese witness swore he remembered Dogan as a little boy, knew his parents and the place they lived in Chinatown. Inspector McCabe was incensed. He knew this to be a lie. But he had no concrete proof. In 1906, a massive earthquake and fire had leveled much of San Francisco, including City Hall, where Chinese birth records were stored.

According to the court transcript for the deportation hearing, the commissioner asked Dogan, "Are you ready to go to war for America?"

Dogan answered, "Sure."

"Will you fight?"

"Yes," he said.

Perhaps the commissioner saw a potential able-bodied soldier standing before him at District Court. In any case, he accepted Dogan's story.
On June 24, 1918, Dogan was conscripted into the US Army and served
as a private in the Medical Department. During a training exercise, he
was injured in his left thigh by shrapnel. He was honorably discharged
on January 13, 1919, two months after the war ended, and returned to
Portland, where he now owned a laundry.

Because Dogan had legal standing as an American citizen, he was
allowed to travel back to China and then reenter the United States with
a wife. But one year passed, then two, and still he didn't return for Toy
Len. During that time, in addition to keeping up with her household
responsibilities, she sewed a trousseau. A gifted seamstress, she made
cotton trousers and tunics as well as more formal outfits of silk—using
hundreds, maybe thousands, of tiny perfect stitches—as questions about
the future, like shiny threads, spooled and unspooled in her mind.

When her mother-in-law died, Toy Len sold the Goon family's final
parcel of land for five hundred silver pieces, which she spent on a lavish
funeral. Village people praised her for this, but to Toy Len it just felt
right. The furniture that had split the house into two sections was now
removed so that Toy Len and her aunt-by-marriage lived in harmony
together. Toy Len stayed on, caring for the children, awaiting Dogan's
return from America. He still seemed in no hurry until one of his childhood friends, Sing Bon, happened to travel from Boston back to Tong
Tow. There he met Toy Len. On his return, he told Dogan that she was
not only beautiful but also respectful of tradition. "Hurry up and bring
that woman to America!" he said.

Sing Bon was so enthusiastic about Toy Len that he even offered to
run the laundry for up to six months while Dogan was away, and Dogan
followed his advice. In Tong Tow, in July of 1921, the couple finally met
and had a second more official wedding, since Toy Len's entry to America required documented proof of marriage. During the five months it

took to assemble all of the travel documents, Toy Len arranged for the children, Doo Ngui and Hung Gee, to stay on with Dogan's aunt in the Goon family home after she and Dogan left for America. (She would continue to send money back to China to pay for their care.)

Finally, on November 10, 1921, Dogan and Toy Len set sail from Hong Kong aboard the SS *Empress of Asia*, bound for Vancouver, Canada. Picture Toy Len, wearing a blue cotton outfit or one of the silk ones, a lovely bride with her handsome husband, leaving the shores of Guangdong forever—her home, her language, her culture. From Vancouver they rode a train to Montreal, then another to Boston. By the time they arrived, thirty-year-old Toy Len was pregnant. Before traveling to Portland, a hundred miles up the coast, they had to pass through the East Boston Immigration Station, New England's equivalent of New York's Ellis Island or San Francisco's Angel Island.

The Chinese Exclusion Act of 1882 was still the law. Incoming Chinese, unlike other immigrants, were quarantined in crowded, prison-like conditions. The Immigration Station, a yellow brick building surrounded by chain-link fence topped with razor wire, offered a grim welcome to America. It was early December, and a cold damp wind blew off the North Atlantic.

Toy Len and Dogan were separated. She was sent to the women's barracks, he to the men's. As an American citizen, Dogan was released the next morning, but Toy Len remained in custody for ten days while her paperwork was scrutinized. Through an interpreter, an immigration officer interrogated her. But she could neither read the documents in Chinese nor speak a word of English.

In the barracks at night, women and children crowded onto three-decker bunks made of wooden planks. Hopes ran high, but so did suffering. Authorities admitted some of the immigrants into the United States, but others, without any means of support or in poor health after the rigors of a long voyage, were deported. As frightening as Toy Len's detention was, she also must have felt lucky. Dogan brought her food from Chinatown every day, which she shared with the others. Once released, they headed to Portland.

Toy Len immersed herself in learning the hand-laundry business and adapted quickly to her new American life. Using a sewing machine Dogan had bought for her, she made herself Western-style housedresses and aprons. For some sixty-five years after her trans-Pacific crossing on the SS *Empress of Asia*, the Chinese outfits she'd sewed by hand lay carefully folded, and unworn, in a cardboard box.

The Goons' first child, a boy named Carroll, was born on May 5, 1922. A few months later, Clara Soule, who taught English and Americanization to immigrants, visited Toy Len and urged her to attend classes. But Toy Len only smiled, gestured at the baby, and shook her head. In spite of differences in language and culture, she and Clara struck up a lasting friendship.

Just a year after Carroll's birth, another son, Richard, appeared. Toy Len soon told Dogan that there needed to be two years between offspring. And so the children came, a total of eight between 1922 and 1936, a span of just fourteen years: Carroll, Richard, Edward, Albert, Josephine, Arthur, Doris, and finally Janet, who was the only one born in a hospital.

Because the family was forced to move twice during their early years, Toy Len hoped to buy a building so they would no longer be at a landlord's mercy. But Dogan balked: They didn't have the money for a down payment. "I'll borrow it from a friend," Toy Len said. Unbeknownst to him, though, ever the frugal manager, she had saved up $500. It was enough for a down payment on a three-story clapboard building in the suburban Woodford's Corner section of Portland at 615 Forest Avenue, where the children would spend most of their formative years.

The first floor held the storefront laundry as well as the family's kitchen and dining area. The second floor was devoted exclusively to bedrooms. For extra income, Toy Len rented out a third-floor apartment. Dogan bought a Studebaker and drove to Boston's Chinatown to buy Chinese herbal medicines and special vegetables unavailable in Portland. He was among the first Chinese in Maine to have a driver's license.

Running a laundry was a hot and physically taxing business, especially at first when most of the jobs were done by hand. Toy Len and Dogan worked side by side. They owned an electric washing machine, but the crank of its mangle was manually operated. At night, clothes hung from the ceiling on wires above the pot-bellied stove. A door sealed off that area so the little drying room heated up. In the morning, clothes were ironed, folded, wrapped in brown paper, tied with twine, and sorted for pickup.

As soon as they were able, the children helped out. The youngest checked pockets for cigarettes or coins, the next oldest sorted sheets and pillowcases or separated men's cotton shirts from their celluloid collars. After school, the more grown-up ones ran back and forth from the stove to a long table, carrying hot eight-pound irons for their parents and oldest siblings to use. The family didn't take vacations; the children wore hand-me-downs, and they shared everything. Even at the age of ninety-three, Carroll, the oldest son, said that whenever he sees a candy bar—a rare childhood treat—he still pictures it divided into eight pieces.

In the evening, Toy Len made traditional Chinese dishes and the family sat down together. After supper, the children did their homework. Not having had the chance for schooling herself, she urged them to excel so they wouldn't have to do hard laundry work for life. While many single Chinese men lived in Portland, there were few families; most moved to Boston because they felt isolated, so far from their own community. But Toy Len insisted her family stay. They had a viable business and the children were thriving, though they were the only Chinese Americans in their classrooms. Bright, well-behaved, conscientious, traditional, and eager to learn, they were well-liked by their teachers and classmates. Among themselves, they spoke English. To their parents, they spoke Chinese and used their Chinese names.

Although they had chores to do, the children often played in the dirt area behind the laundry, and the boys occasionally walked down to Deering Oaks Park. At home, this gaggle of eight could be rowdy. But in public, they behaved—always. Doris, the second to youngest, noted that they were all wanted, disciplined, and loved. Toy Len herself also found time to enjoy visits from Clara Soule and made a good friend in Mrs. Kalil, a Syrian who lived above the grocery store next door. In thickly accented "English," the two shared recipes for American food.

In 1938, Dogan developed gangrene. Eventually, his leg was amputated at mid-thigh. The wooden leg doctors fitted him for was uncomfortable, and he never fully recovered. Toy Len ran the business herself while also taking care of her husband and the children. Her intelligence, parenting skills, and business acumen would be tested as never before. She usually worked sixteen-hour days. Understanding that she couldn't do it alone, however, she developed a clever, practical plan. Instead of starting his junior year at nearby Deering High School that fall, the oldest, Carroll, would help her run the laundry for two years so that the second son, Richard, could graduate.

When the Deering principal, Mr. Wiggin, heard of the family's hardships, he arranged for teachers to drop books by the laundry for Carroll to study. Returning to high school two years later, he was an even more focused and successful student than before. He wanted to be a doctor, he told Mr. Wiggin, who was able to arrange a full scholarship to Syracuse University. In this way, the laundry stayed afloat, and all the children graduated from high school. The third son, Edward, was vice president of his senior class at Deering; the fourth son, Albert, was elected senior class president. Years later, Edward remembered that he "sometimes memorized the Latin and French vocabulary lessons while ironing."

Although Toy Len nursed Dogan tenderly, he died on May 3, 1941. It was a terrible spring. In spite of her own grief, she had to keep going. The children, ages five to nineteen, had lost their father, and the family's very survival depended on the laundry. Officials from the City of Portland offered Toy Len financial assistance. "It would better for the children if they don't have to work," they insisted.

Toy Len refused it. "It would be shameful to receive public welfare," she said, "as we'd lose self-respect and be unable to earn our keep, according to Chinese values." The children were her responsibility, and the city's assistance would be less than her laundry's income. In addition, accepting aid meant she'd have to sell their building, the family's only asset, which they had bought and fully paid for two years before Dogan died. "Let's keep the laundry, work together, stay together," she told her children. It was a brave and risky step. Although Toy Len and the children struggled, she still sent money back to China for Doo Ngui and Hung Gee.

In 1943, during World War II, President Franklin D. Roosevelt finally rescinded the Chinese Exclusion Act. By then, Toy Len's eight children were well on their way to higher education and to financial and personal success. Their achievements read like a page taken from *Who's Who*:

> Carroll D. Goon, a graduate of Syracuse University and Johns Hopkins Medical School, was a doctor in Monticello, Utah, for thirty years.
>
> Richard G. Len (Goon) graduated from Rensselaer Polytechnic Institute (RPI) in physics and started his own successful company, RG Len TV and Appliances, which he ran for over thirty years.
>
> Edward J. Guen (Goon) graduated cum laude from Bowdoin College in math and physics, received a BS in chemistry from MIT and a PhD in chemistry from RPI, and completed postdoctoral work at Tufts University.

Albert G. Len (Goon) graduated from Boston University Law School, where he was on the Law Review. After earning a master's in taxation at New York University, he became a tax lawyer and worked in estates and trusts for the New Hampshire Department of Revenue.

Josephine G. Moy graduated from Westbrook Junior College and was a bookkeeper and office manager for her sister Doris's court reporting company.

Arthur Len (Goon) graduated from Tufts University with a BS degree, served in the US Navy, and worked at Digital Equipment Corporation.

Doris O. Wong graduated from the Stenotype Institute of Boston; established her own court reporting company, Doris O. Wong Associates; and was president of the National Court Reporters Association.

Janet Louie graduated from Simmons College with BS and MS degrees. She was a psychiatric social work counselor as well as a director of clinical services.

For an illiterate immigrant mother, the single parent for much of her children's early years, this was a heroic accomplishment. Others have done this and will continue to—immigrants from Ireland and Italy, Southeast Asia, Eastern Europe, Africa, Central and South America. For the most part, however, their sacrifices and resourcefulness are lauded solely within their own families or communities. But for Toy Len Goon, something very different lay in store.

In 1952, her friend Clara Soule asked Toy Len if she'd mind being nominated for State of Maine Mother of the Year. Urged on by her family, Toy Len agreed, though the notion bemused her. In fact, she was well respected among local business owners, neighbors and friends, her children's teachers, and customers at the laundry. Amazing as it seemed to her, she was selected.

But the wonders didn't end there. As a state winner, she was considered for the national award, sponsored by the Mothers Committee of the Golden Rule Society. Out of forty-eight remarkable women, one from each state, the group chose Toy Len Goon. A former Chinese peasant— whose people just nine years before had been barred from entering the United States—was now America's Mother of the Year.

Modest, self-effacing Toy Len handled the ensuing equivalent of a media frenzy with humble dignity. Newspapers in Maine, Boston, and New York wanted to interview her on topics from raising children and running a laundry to cooking lobster, Chinese-style. Soon coverage went national. A newsreel splashed Toy Len's image onto movie screens across the country. In early May, the American Mothers Committee sponsored a luncheon for her at New York City's Waldorf Astoria Hotel. Less than a week later, a crowd of some two thousand lined the streets of New York's Chinatown for a parade in her honor. She stood in the back of a convertible, smartly dressed and smiling, "waving just like Queen Elizabeth," Doris noted.

Next it was on to Washington, DC, where she had lunch in the dining room of the Speaker of the United States House of Representatives. She visited the White House, hosted by First Lady Bess Truman. She and all her children except for Carroll, who was doctoring in Utah, were photographed on the steps of the United States Capitol. Parades also greeted Toy Len in Chinatowns in Boston and Philadelphia. Before leaving home, she had worried about her laundry customers, but the head of the largest laundry company in Portland promised to keep her service on schedule.

The festivities continued into June, including teas, luncheons, and celebrations organized by fellow businesspeople and city officials in Portland. Vallee's Restaurant, located in Woodford's Corner, hosted the Goon family for dinner. It was their first time eating out, and Doris and Janet joked giddily about which fork to use.

Toy Len's selection as 1952's Mother of the Year coincided with the height of the Korean War. The United States was fighting on the side of South Korea against the North, which was backed by the People's Republic of China and the Soviet Union. Both sides were also waging a propaganda war. The People's Republic publicized America's racist persecution of Asian immigrants, highlighting the Chinese Exclusion Act. The choice of Toy Len Goon as America's Mother of the Year, then, played well.

Chiang Kai-shek, president of the Republic of China on Taiwan and a US ally, embraced her success. He invited her to visit Taipei as his guest and sent her a scroll, which he had reputedly painted himself. And the Nationalist Chinese ambassador, Wellington Koo, and his wife entertained her. For all her propaganda value, however, Toy Len Goon was nobody's pawn. She richly deserved every honor she received; the power of her story was compelling.

Although Toy Len soon returned to her work in Portland, hand laundries were losing business. During World War II, smaller, cheaper, more efficient motors had been perfected, putting home washing machines within reach of the growing middle class, and coin-operated Laundromats opened around the city.

Meanwhile, Toy Len's children encouraged her to retire and let them take care of her. That same year, 1952, she closed the laundry, rented the building, and moved to Lynn, Massachusetts, where her son Richard lived. The youngest, Janet, graduated from Lynn-English High School. When her daughter Doris bought a condo in Swampscott, on Boston's North Shore, Toy Len moved in and remained there for some thirty years. By then all of her children had achieved her dreams for them: They were well educated, successful, and had families of their own.

Toy Len was far from idle during the last decades of her life. She did much of the taking-care: cooking, cleaning, and helping to raise some of her grandchildren. During that time she converted to Christianity and became a naturalized American citizen. An avid Boston sports fan, she tuned the TV to Bruins hockey games to watch her favorite player, Bobby Orr. She also enjoyed the soap opera *General Hospital*.

Family remained the focus for Toy Len, and three generations flocked around her. She was the guiding force, the role model, the moral compass. She liked hearing details about their lives, not only laughing at toddler antics but listening seriously to stories about schools, workplaces, salaries. She didn't hesitate to give advice. It was direct, sometimes pointed, but always given with gentleness, humor, and love.

In addition to family, Toy Len had two other visitors whose efforts to see her moved her deeply. One was Mrs. Kalil, her old neighbor at Woodford's Corner. Mrs. Kalil had also left Portland and lived with one of her children somewhere in the Midwest. When she was asked if there was anything she'd like to do before she died, she said, "Yes, I'd like to visit Mrs. Goon." The other visitor rose up from the much more distant past—a man from the family she'd served in Gan Cun, starting when she was only ten. No doubt he must have heard news of her American Mother of the Year Award and tracked her down. He came to tell how much he had admired and appreciated her all those years ago. In their native Taishanese, a dialect of Cantonese, they spoke not as master and servant but as equals.

Toy Len died peacefully on May 27, 1993, just a few months shy of her 102nd birthday. Thanks to the efforts of her children and grandchildren, and a Portland lawyer and historian, Gary Libby, an exhibition of Goon family artifacts was mounted at the Maine Historical Society in 2004. These included some of Toy Len's hand-sewn silk outfits, which textile expert Jacqueline Field had the chance to examine. She was amazed at the fine stitching and even more amazed by the silk itself. It was an unusual type called "mud silk" because during the finishing process it was washed in a river, whose silt gave it a lovely dark sheen. In 2012, the family donated two of these mud silk outfits to the

Smithsonian Institution in Washington, DC. One was exhibited at the Smithsonian's National Museum of American History in 2014.

While Toy Len herself did not wish to return to China, some of her children did visit her husband's childhood village Tong Tow. They helped finance a school for girls and boys that was built there, and dedicated in honor of a little girl who began life carrying buckets of water on a shoulder pole and honoring spirits. Toy Len's own spirit still illuminates and guides her many descendants: eight children, twenty-four grandchildren, and forty-six great-grandchildren.

FLORENCE EASTMAN WILLIAMS

———•◦•———

(1892–1984)

Working Woman, Clairvoyant, Beloved Matriarch

In 1943, in the middle of World War II, times were hard in Portland, Maine. But at night in the USO Club near the waterfront, Big Band dance music and the sound of laughter filled the air. The club was a bright light for young soldiers and sailors heading to Europe on transport ships anchored in Portland harbor. And one of the brightest lights there was Florence Williams.

Florence, nicknamed Flossie, was fifty-one, a hard-working woman with a family to support, ever since she and her husband had separated. But, looking at her, you'd never know she had a single care. She was a buoyant spirit, with beautiful dark eyes and long black hair. Only four feet ten inches with size 2½ shoes—always very high heels—she was a dynamo. As a hostess at the club, she greeted new arrivals, served refreshments, and danced with the servicemen, many barely out of their teens. They called her "Mom Williams." Those evenings, her most important task—and pleasure—was talking to these kids about home: their families, girlfriends, dreams. She joked and made them smile; she admired their photos and listened to their worries as well as their hopes. Throughout the war, she invited one or two of them to Sunday dinner at her house on Anderson Street. Because food was rationed, it was a stretch to feed so many. But at her table, everyone was welcome, all backgrounds, all races.

Florence Eastman Williams (far right) with two of her sisters Courtesy June
McKenzie and family

"Thanks, Mom," they'd say when they left the Williamses' house, hearts gladdened and bellies full of fried chicken.

But June, Flossie's fourteen-year-old, would feel hopping mad. "She's not your mom, she's mine," she would snap.

Now a woman in her eighties, June McKenzie just laughs and shakes her head at her teenage jealousy, the way her mother must have done more than seventy years ago. Long after World War II ended, the same young men who appreciated Mom Williams's hospitality continued to correspond with her, and if they happened to visit Portland again, they made sure to stop by Anderson Street. Flossie's love for people and her ability to empathize led to a lifelong penchant for inclusion, even when she herself might feel excluded.

Florence Eastman was born in Portland on September 15, 1892, one of Annie Barnett and George M. Eastman's five daughters. Long-time Portland residents, Annie's family was originally from Dutch Guyana (now Suriname), on the northern coast of South America, where family members owned a railroad and had other landholdings. Before moving to Portland, the Barnetts lived in Portsmouth, New Hampshire, for a few years. In the early decades of the 1800s, when they most likely arrived in Portland, its docks teemed with commercial fishing boats and clipper ships. Granite, lumber, and manufactured goods—all moved to and from the city's docks. A small but cosmopolitan African-American community, including many seamen who worked on sailing ships, grew up around India and Fore Streets, near the eastern end of the waterfront.

Flossie's family lived on Anderson Street at the base of Munjoy Hill, half a mile from the waterfront, in a house just "down the yard" from her paternal grandparents, Charles and Harriet Eastman. A short cement walkway, lined with forsythia, hollyhocks, and hydrangeas, led from one house to the other. From her grandparents Flossie learned family history, from the days when Charles Eastman was the clerk at the Abyssinian Church, built in 1828. Still standing today on Newbury Street, the Church is Maine's oldest—and the nation's third-oldest—African-American meetinghouse. In the decades before the Civil War, not only was it the only school for black children, it was also a "safe haven" on the Underground Railroad.

No doubt Flossie heard stories about the Railroad from her grandfather, such as the one involving a runaway slave whom he helped deliver to freedom. Charles drove a hack in Portland—a horse and buggy taxi. He also was a barber and a taxidermist; in addition, he sometimes worked at the Portland Club. The fleeing slave, pursued by his former owners and by the police, was smuggled out of the South on a ship bound for Portland. Although Maine (part of Massachusetts until 1820) had abolished slavery in 1783, the year the Revolutionary War ended, it was still against the law to harbor a fugitive slave from another state. In spite of this law—and the great danger associated with breaking it—Charles Eastman drove his hack late at night to the Portland Club, where abolitionists had hidden the man once he was sneaked off the ship. Charles helped the fugitive into his buggy's secret compartment, then traveled across town to the Abyssinian Church until arrangements could be made to spirit him across the Canadian border. This type of compassionate action influenced young Florence greatly.

Flossie grew up at the end of the nineteenth and the beginning of the twentieth centuries. Around 1900, Maine—"this whitest part of the country"—had a population of approximately 700,000, of whom only 1,300 were African-American. Her father, George Eastman, followed in his father Charles's footsteps. He drove a hack, did taxidermy, and owned a barbershop on India Street, serving members of the black community, unwelcome at white barbershops. Although racism was more subtle than in the South, rules of segregation were still clear and boundaries were carefully watched. At that time schools were open to all children, but there was prejudice in housing, employment, and social opportunities. The Eastmans owned their own homes, so Flossie grew up not knowing that kind of discrimination.

As a girl, Flossie was taught to sew, do fancy handwork, and cook. She was a diligent worker and talented with her hands. She went to North School on the top of Munjoy Hill, graduating from the eighth grade in 1905. That ended her formal schooling. During her childhood she attended both the Abyssinian Church, whose membership was dwindling, and the newer Mission, part of the African Methodist Episcopal (AME) Zion Church, founded in 1891. (The Abyssinian closed in 1917, when Flossie was twenty-five.)

Flossie was the middle of five sisters. Annie and Alice were older, Gertrude and Irene younger. Gertrude died of "quick consumption" during a flu epidemic when she was only eighteen. All of the girls except Flossie were very fair skinned, and she believed that her mother favored them because of this. In fact, Flossie felt that her mother didn't like her at all, but she adored—and was adored by—her father and her grandparents. In spite of her mother's harshness, Flossie was a happy child—bubbly, warm, and funny.

In 1912, Flossie fell in love with Mitchell Williams, also a Portland native. He'd attended Tuskegee Institute, an African-American university in Alabama, where he'd trained to be a mechanic. He owned his own garage, but Flossie's parents still disapproved of him. She believed this was because he was darker skinned than her own family. Nevertheless, the couple decided to marry in December of 1912. Flossie was twenty. Without her parents in attendance, the wedding took place at the AME Zion Church, now called Green Memorial. After the ceremony, Flossie went home to gather up her belongings; she found them on the front stoop, wrapped in newspaper.

At first the young couple lived on Portland's West End, but after Flossie's parents reconciled to her marriage, she and Mitchell moved to the family's Anderson Street house. Their first child, Dorothy (called

Dot), was born in 1913, followed by four more girls: Edith in 1915, Eleanor about 1917, Helen in 1919, and Audrey about 1921. Next came Mitchell Jr., who died in infancy. George Eastman Williams, called Sonny, was born in 1925. During her next labor, a difficult one, hospital staff didn't treat Flossie in time and the baby died with the cord wrapped around his neck—the result of medical neglect perhaps caused by discriminatory attitudes. Flossie gave birth to a daughter, June, in October of 1929, followed by another son, also named Mitchell Jr., in 1933. The last children, a set of twins, Jean and Joan, came in 1935, when Flossie was forty-three. Both died during a flu epidemic, one at ten weeks, one at ten months. Less than two years later, her fifth daughter, Audrey, died at the age of sixteen. Of Flossie's twelve children, only seven lived into adulthood. Although her heart was broken repeatedly, she expressed no bitterness. She refused to dwell on what she'd lost; she simply carried on.

Flossie created happy childhoods for her kids. Her home was a center of activity, always full of children, her own as well as others. She was a great cook and sewed all the girls' clothes, making muffs and coats, doing fine embroidery. Her kids attended North School as she had done, and all of them graduated from Portland High School. When they were little, they walked home for lunch to find fresh biscuits baking. She would be outside, waiting, chatting with her neighbors over the back fence: Irish, Polish, and Italian immigrants. Hers was the only black family in a diverse neighborhood, but Florence was a friend to all. "She never said a bad word about anybody," June recalls. When the Karolewskis, Polish neighbors, went for their citizenship papers, Flossie stood up for them.

Flossie was a terrific domestic manager, creating a loving but strict household. She ruled with a natural, quiet authority, with love, laughter, and firm rules. You helped with chores, you learned to share. Dinner was always at 6:00 p.m. "Be there," and the children were. Flossie never hit any of them and her reprimands were slight when anybody acted up: "Behave" and "Be nice" were her favorites.

While Mitchell told the kids, "If anyone calls you anything but your name, smack him," their mother would disagree. "No," she'd say, "that's not right."

From childhood on, Flossie knew that she possessed an unusual gift: clairvoyance. Well known and well respected for her ability to predict the future, she refused to take money when friends and neighbors came to her kitchen asking her to read their tea leaves. Even strangers would knock on her door and beg for her guidance. Sometimes the gift must have felt like a burden. Her face would change. She'd see a bright light shining on the wall. "Something's going to happen," she'd say.

Once, after Mitchell had taken up long-distance trucking, she ordered one of the kids to go to the garage and "tell your dad to look between the truck and the cab, something's not right with the coupling."

"You've got to hurry!" she once told June, sending her off running to the same garage. Flossie could see Mitchell, plain as day, climbing out of his truck after it burst into flames. But June arrived too late to stop him. The truck did catch fire. Luckily, Mitchell escaped through a cab window, just as Flossie had witnessed it in her mind's eye.

Growing up, her children sometimes found their mother's clairvoyance annoying, but they learned to trust her instincts.

"You don't want to do that," she'd tell one of them.

"Why?"

"Listen to me. You don't want to do that." And invariably she was right.

June remembers her mother saying "Uh-oh" out of the blue. "Somebody's coming here and it's not good." Sometimes it might be the police, sometimes a friend was sick. Because they didn't always have a phone, most news—good or bad—came through the side door.

During the Depression, the Williamses struggled, as did almost every other family. In the summers, they'd move to Scarborough, then a rural area about ten miles south of Portland, where they owned a few acres. They lived in a small trailer on a beautiful parcel of land and had a regular farm with a cow, pigs, and chickens. Flossie planted a huge vegetable garden, whose abundant harvest she canned and preserved. The kids helped to hoe and weed. Late in the summer, before school started, the pigs would be slaughtered so there'd be meat through the winter.

Mitchell especially loved the farm, but it was hard for Flossie because she didn't drive and felt isolated, far from her Portland friends and church community. About 1940, when Flossie was forty-eight, Mitchell decided to stay in Scarborough year-round, while she returned to Anderson Street. Although the couple separated, they never divorced.

Mitchell still visited the kids, but now Flossie needed to support the family largely on her own. These were tough, lean, lonely times, but she kept her spirits high for her children and for the young servicemen at the USO Club where she soon found a job. The older set of kids were now mostly in their twenties—the youngest of that group, Sonny, was fifteen. June was only eleven and Mitchell Jr., called Skippy, was seven. To feed them, Flossie took all kinds of jobs, all physically grueling, some of the few available to black women. In addition to working at the USO in the evenings, rolling bandages and teaching dance routines to a girls' youth group there, she cleaned houses for wealthy people during the day, and late at night scrubbed floors and cleaned bathrooms at Scarborough Downs Racetrack.

Most of Flossie's children grew up and moved away, but June remained in Portland near her mother. While June was raising her own family, Flossie lived upstairs and helped take care of the kids so June could work. The grandchildren adored "Nanie." She was a powerful force, a grounding, a pole star. For a number of years, she shared a room with her granddaughter, Michele, who now observes that while most teenage girls might resent such an arrangement, she loved it because Nanie was such a supportive and positive woman.

Another granddaughter, Merita, remembers the afternoon ritual of drinking tea with milk or cream in the kitchen with Nanie, who "could see pictures in the tea leaves left in the bottom of the cup." A second mother to June's children, Nanie also had a wonderful sense of fun. She liked to dance, recalls Merita. "She would call herself 'dancing-a-jig.' She was so cute to watch. Standing about four feet ten inches, she would grab the edge of her skirt and hold it up while she shuffled and kicked her high-heeled feet."

When Flossie had a spare minute, she liked to play the card game whist with her friends, and she was an avid member of an all-black women's group, the Misteray Club. She was also very involved with the Green Memorial Church. As a member of the Missionary Board, she collected food, visited the sick, and took care of the community's elderly. Not long after a 1965 fire at June's house, Flossie moved to Franklin Towers, a subsidized housing complex, to keep her sister Alice and niece Shirley company. By that time, in her seventies, Flossie had retired from the heavy domestic work she had always hated.

As the years passed, she remained youthful, the center of activity for her ever-expanding family. Well into her seventies, she took up ceramics and made lighted ceramic Christmas trees for all of her children and adult grandchildren. Her hair didn't turn gray until she was about eighty-seven. June, who worked at a bank, would walk home to see her mother every day. "If I was feeling down, she'd cheer me up."

"Nanie lived a long life well," her granddaughter Michele says. "She loved loving other people, and she loved being loved." Merita notes that her grandmother's gifts were enduring ones. "Nanie taught me that, no matter what, I was a child of God, and that He loved me and so did she. She taught me that I had worth, and that I should take pride in myself. She often told me that 'we came from royalty in Dutch Guyana.'"

On the morning of June 7, 1984, Florence Eastman Williams felt sick when she woke up. She died that same day, at the age of ninety-one. "Small in stature, big in heart" read one of her obituaries. Nicknamed "Mom Williams" by servicemen during World War II, she was truly everyone's mother. For her, race didn't matter, nor did ethnic background or social class. She was a strong, strong person who accepted that you alter your dreams as you go along. While her life wasn't easy, she refused to dwell on the negative. "How can we move forward?" was both her challenge and her legacy.

Sister R. Mildred Barker

(1897–1990)

"Hands to Work, Hearts to God"

In 1903, when Mildred Barker was only six, her father died suddenly, shattering the family and dramatically changing the arc of her future. Mildred's mother, unable to care for her two children, sent her son off to a trade school and placed Mildred at Holy Land, a Shaker community in Alfred, Maine. In the early twentieth century, it was relatively common for the Shakers to take in orphans or, like Mildred, the children of destitute parents. At the time there was no Aid for Dependent Children, no federal, state, or local agency to help needy families.

Overnight then, the Shaker brothers and sisters became Mildred's new family. One of her favorites at Holy Land was an elderly sister named Paulina Springer, whom she loved dearly. Sister Paulina taught Shaker hymns and songs to Mildred. Even at a young age, Mildred had a natural aptitude for singing and a wonderful memory. She was quick, bright, and wiry, with big brown eyes that didn't miss a beat. And keen ears that didn't miss a beat, either. After listening once or twice to a song then singing along, she'd memorize both lyrics and melody. Mildred seemed to soak up songs at a gulp, the way thirsty soil soaks up rain. She also delighted in learning the pantomime gestures that often accompanied the older hymns.

Sister Mildred Barker United Society of Shakers, Sabbathday Lake, Inc.

As Sister Paulina's health deteriorated, Mildred was assigned to help tidy her room and wait on her. "It was my greatest delight to do it," Mildred said years later, "because I thought she was just an angel, nothing else." Soon, Sister Paulina was too weak to leave her bed, but her spirit remained loving and strong. At age ninety, she wasn't sick with any particular disease, she was just simply fading away. One September morning, close to the end, she asked to see the children, who visited her bedroom one by one. Mildred came last. Frail as she was, Sister Paulina smiled at Mildred and squeezed her hand. "Promise me you'll be a Shaker," she said.

Growing up Shaker didn't necessarily mean you would adopt the Shaker faith in adulthood. At twenty-one, you had a choice: You were free to leave the community or sign the Shaker Covenant and remain. Mildred was too young to grasp any of this, but she would have done anything Sister Paulina asked, and so, of course, she promised. After Mildred left the room, Paulina told one of her fellow sisters, "I'm not going to be here much longer. Two angels standing over by the cupboard door are waiting for me." She died a short time later.

It would take Mildred many years to truly understand what her promise meant and to fulfill it. Although she was only eight when Sister Paulina died, the elderly Shaker exerted a powerful influence lasting to the end of Sister Mildred's own long and remarkable life. Out of the thousands of Shaker songs Sister Mildred knew by heart, one with special significance would always be "Mother Has Come with Her Beautiful Song," which Sister Paulina had taught her so long ago. This was a "gift song," given to Sister Paulina by a tiny bird. The "mother" the song refers to is the founder of the Shakers, Mother Ann Lee, and it was her teachings that shaped Mildred Barker's life, giving it profound spiritual purpose and meaning.

Ann Lee, born in Manchester, England, in 1736, was the daughter of a blacksmith. During her marriage, she bore four children, all of whom died. From an early age, Ann was "endowed with uncommonly deep religious feelings," Sister Mildred would write many years later in her book *The Sabbathday Shakers: An Introduction to the Shaker Heritage.* Ann Lee joined a small religious group in Manchester, led by James and Jane Wardley. This society was called, derisively, "Shaking Quakers" and then simply "Shakers" "because of their ecstatic and violent bodily agitation" during worship. Sister Mildred wrote that Ann Lee, while under the guidance of the Wardleys, "became more deeply inspired and was blessed with divine insight, revelations and prophecies." Soon the group naturally turned to her for leadership and advice.

But in England Ann Lee and her followers were bitterly persecuted for their beliefs. She herself was beaten, stoned, and often put in prison. In 1770, she received a revelation to go to America. Because they were so poor, it took four years before Mother Ann and eight followers could raise enough money to pay the ship's passage. They left Liverpool, England, on May 19, 1774, in a condemned vessel, the *Maria*, arriving in New York two and a half months later, on August 6, 1774.

The United Society of Believers in Christ's Second Appearing wanted to return to the simplicity of the early Christian church, believing that Christ's second coming lived within each individual. To the Shakers, "God is the First Great Cause. God is all, including the source of the Christ life spirit." Theirs were radical beliefs. One hundred fifty years before American women gained the vote, seventy-five years before the Emancipation Proclamation, the Shakers practiced equality in every realm of life: social, racial, economic, and spiritual. They shared all property and lived celibate lives. They also were pacifists, to whom Abraham Lincoln gave conscientious objector status during the Civil War. Each Shaker community was governed by two women and two men, called Eldresses and Elders.

By the time Mildred's mother brought her to Holy Land, the number of Shakers in the society had been declining for more than fifty years. At its height in the 1840s, more than six thousand members had lived in nineteen communal villages in New York, New England, and from Ohio and Indiana to Kentucky. The Shakers inspired many other utopian attempts—social experiments which tried to create ideal communities. They have endured the longest.

Ruth Jackson, Mildred's mother, had been raised a Catholic in Manchester, England, where Mother Ann Lee had lived before she came to America. It is not known exactly when Ruth herself came to the United States, but she married Mildred's father, James Powell Barker, an Episcopalian, whose own family had roots in Rhode Island. The couple settled in Providence. Here Ruth Mildred was born on February 3, 1897. She had an older brother, and there was also a younger sister, but she died in infancy. After James Barker's sudden death, grief swallowed Ruth, who had no means to support her young children.

Ruth had a cousin who had joined a Shaker community in southern Maine, and it was there, by prior arrangement, that she took Mildred by train on July 7, 1903. It was a blistering hot afternoon when the train stopped in the middle of a cow pasture, surrounded by hills. Driving a horse and wagon, Brother Stephen picked up the two and delivered them to a cluster of large houses across the field. In the office of Eldress Fannie Casey, Ruth Barker signed a paper called an indenture, meaning that the Shakers would now be Mildred's family. Ruth returned to Providence on the next train, leaving her daughter behind.

The sisters were kind and welcoming. They showed Mildred her new home and introduced her to the fourteen other girls with whom she would share a single bedroom in the Dwelling House. But she was terribly homesick. She just couldn't understand why her mother had abandoned her. For several days she'd walk out behind the Dwelling House alone to gaze out across the hills. Providence lay just over the hills, she thought, and she planned to run away, back to her mother, her brother, her home.

In spite of the first traumatic days, Mildred quickly adapted to her new life. Soon she felt both wanted and loved. Of Eldress Harriett Coolbroth, her caretaker, she later wrote, "She was the mother that I needed, and as a young child I thought there couldn't possibly be anyone any lovelier." Almost every night before bed, she would go to

Eldress Harriett Coolbroth's room, where she learned Shaker songs. One of the first ones began with the words: "Come, little children, come to Zion. Come, little children, march along."

Often, as the months and years went by, Mildred would stop sisters while they worked—in the sewing rooms, in the laundry and kitchen—to ask them to teach her songs. Years later she said, "It was almost a passion with me to see how many I could learn." Mildred's was a happy childhood as she learned not only to read and write but to do all kinds of useful housekeeping and homemaking chores, including knitting, sewing, spinning, embroidering, and jelly-making.

The Shaker motto was "Hands to work, hearts to God," and Holy Land was a bustling enterprise, as well as a peaceful place of worship and prayer. To supplement their farming income, the Shakers made "anything we could sell." In the summer, an elder would visit resort hotels at nearby beaches or in the White Mountains, where wealthy vacationers bought such "fancy-goods" as poplar boxes, long cloaks, and hand-knitted sweaters. No matter what the product—from chairs and tables to mail-order packaged seeds, dried herbs, and lady's sewing baskets—the Shaker name meant top-quality workmanship, since Believers strove for perfection in all they did. Shakers were also known for their creativity. Flat brooms, clothespins, metal-point pens, circular saws, washing machines, early wrinkle-resistant fabrics—all were invented by Shakers intent on finding more efficient, labor-saving ways to perform their daily tasks.

Although Mildred's formal education ended with the eighth grade, she was an avid member of the Beacon Light Club. At weekly meetings she continued to read literature, learn history, and write essays and poetry, which she loved. She also enjoyed cooking. In fact, while still only in her teens, she was a head cook at Holy Land.

For years, Mildred didn't hear a word from her mother. Then, in 1913, when Mildred was sixteen, Ruth reappeared. She'd been remarried and wanted her daughter to come home with her. But Mildred refused. The Shakers were her family and Holy Land her home. Surprisingly, perhaps, Ruth agreed to this, understanding how deeply her daughter loved the Shakers, so different from "the world's people," as they called non-Shakers. The two visited often and remained close until Ruth's death in 1951.

In 1918, when Mildred turned twenty-one, she signed the Church Covenant, the first step in fulfilling the promise she'd made to Sister Paulina Springer years before. Throughout these years, the Shakers' numbers continued to dwindle, as fewer and fewer of the "world's people" converted. In 1931, the Alfred community was forced to close. Thirty-four-year-old Sister Mildred and twenty other brothers and sisters moved to "Chosen Land," a Shaker community at Sabbathday Lake, Maine, founded in 1783. Mildred would live there for almost sixty years.

Although she hadn't quite recovered from a serious illness late in the 1930s, Sister Mildred embraced a new and sizable challenge at Chosen Land: She took the community's teenage girls under her wing. Being in charge of ten girls' physical and spiritual well-being consumed her energies, but she thrived on the responsibility. Sister Frances Carr, in her wonderful memoir, *Growing Up Shaker*, credits Sister Mildred with creating a happy and productive entry into womanhood for herself and many other girls. "We never experienced anything except a great deal of patience, love and kindness from her," wrote Sister Frances. Whether the girls chose to remain Shakers as adults or not, many called Sister Mildred "mother" and visited her as often as they could in later life.

No doubt remembering her own teenage years, Sister Mildred loved the girls, made them laugh, helped them learn, and kept them busy. In her memoir, Sister Frances tells a story about testing Sister Mildred. On the first night at the Dwelling House, after moving up from the Children's House, Frances avoided answering Sister Mildred's question about whether or not she'd said her prayers. Sister Mildred expressed neither surprise nor anger; she simply asked, "Would you like to say them with me?" Thus began a tradition that would last for fifty years.

Sister Mildred had a gift for making work-time fun. Even during lean years, Sister Frances recalled, Sister Mildred would turn an evening's sewing tasks into a party—with Kool-Aid and sandwiches made of ground-up Spam, cut into festive shapes. On birthdays, she whipped up rich chocolate cakes. One Christmas, she sewed housecoats for her girls in their favorite colors. A talented seamstress, she made thousands of potholders and hundreds of aprons to sell at the Shaker store. Every Friday evening, she taught the girls Shaker songs, passing on the oral tradition she had lovingly cultivated, and on Saturday afternoons, she enjoyed listening to opera on the radio while she sewed or knitted.

When the fancy-goods business fell off because of the Great Depression—which coincided with Sister Mildred's arrival at Chosen Land—she proposed that the Shakers start up another money-making industry: candy. She and Sister Jenny convinced the society to invest $1,000 on state-of-the-art equipment, and they studied the candy-making process in Portland. Soon, the Shakers were making and selling thirty-one different varieties—from taffy to filled chocolates, which Sister Mildred hand-dipped herself. Candy production reached its height in 1941, but then fell off during World War II when sugar was strictly rationed. Sister Mildred's jellies and jams were always highly prized, and she was known to be fussy about ingredients. Right before picking time, she would stride through Chosen Land's bountiful orchards to select the apples she wanted for pectin.

In 1950, Sister Mildred, then fifty-three, was chosen to succeed Sister Prudence as a trustee of the Shaker community, a position she held until she died. As such, she was both a spiritual and a temporal leader. She also wrote three books and many articles about Shaker life. Soon she was traveling around the country, giving lectures and serving as a Shaker ambassador to the "world's people." As the Shakers' numbers decreased, she sometimes grew tired of questions about the future of the United Society of Believers, but she was always gracious. With wry humor she once said to a reporter, "When people tell me, 'Oh, you're a Shaker. You make all that lovely furniture,' I feel like a table or a chair." Shakerism, she made very clear, was more than a beautiful chair or a quaint white cap.

Humble and modest, Sister Mildred didn't boast about her accomplishments. In telling her life story to interviewer Ann Waldron, for example, she left out that she'd met composer Aaron Copland in Cleveland when he was celebrating his ninetieth birthday. *Appalachian Spring*, Copland's famous ballet commissioned for Martha Graham, included several variations of the Shaker melody "Simple Gifts," and he had been eager to learn its history from Sister Mildred.

In June of 1983, the National Endowment for the Arts invited Sister Mildred to Washington, DC. At a gala ceremony, she and fifteen other outstanding folk artists—among them blues singer and guitarist John Lee Hooker—received National Heritage Fellowship Awards. Hers, given for her mastery of Shaker music, was presented by renowned folk singer Pete Seeger. Sister Mildred was eighty-six years old. Inspired by the event, she surprised the audience with an unplanned rendition of Sister Paulina's "Mother Has Come with Her Beautiful Song." While in Washington, she also sang at the Smithsonian. Many of these songs had never been written down or preserved on tape until she recorded them. Interviewed by the *Washington Post* for a story about the National Heritage award, Sister Mildred said:

> *I'm just an ordinary singer. I never had a big training, mine is just the spirit, that's all. I didn't realize for a very long time how important it was, it was a feeling I got myself from the old songs, the music. It suddenly came upon me that I was keeping the tradition alive, which meant everything to me.*

When Sister Frances Carr was asked to describe Sister Mildred for an article in *National Geographic* magazine, she said of her beloved mentor, caretaker, and friend, "She is the most perfect Shaker I have known. [She] epitomizes Shaker values: compassion, love, total dedication. No compromises here. She is rigorous, a drill sergeant of the soul."

Sister Mildred herself, quoted in the *Maine Sunday Telegram*, reflected on the discipline, strength, and spiritual devotion needed to "take up the Cross." Perhaps she was thinking of her long-ago promise to Sister Paulina Springer when she said, "We have to work for it. It takes years to do it. . . . It means transforming your whole life."

Sister Mildred died on January 25, 1990, at the age of ninety-three. She is buried in the communal Shaker cemetery at Sabbathday Lake. Chosen Land, believed to be the oldest continuously operating religious community in the United States, is still an active Shaker village. Four sisters and brothers keep up Shaker traditions on their 1,800 acres of rolling hills, orchards, fields, and pasturelands. At their store, they sell books, CDs, herbs, and crafts, and guides give comprehensive tours of the historic meetinghouse and grounds. The Shaker library, formerly the schoolhouse, is open by appointment to scholars, researchers, and any others seeking to learn about the Shakers and their many gifts to the world.

And what of the future? "We're just a small group," Sister Mildred once said, "but it's something that the world needs and I'm sure it's going to pass right down through many centuries. I don't believe that it will be lost. We can use all the strength and all the faith that we have and keep it alive and pass it to those who come within our reach. It's God's work, and He will sustain it."

MARGARET CHASE SMITH

(1897–1995)

"A Ship's Figurehead in Proud Profile"

On June 1, 1950, the junior senator from Maine, Margaret Chase Smith, rose to address her colleagues. "I may not have the courage to do this," she'd told a trusted aide earlier that day, but there she was, the lone woman in the Senate, poised to speak her mind, and her conscience.

At the time of her speech, the United States was consumed with anti-Communist crusading, whipped to excess by Wisconsin Senator Joseph R. McCarthy. At first, Smith had supported her fellow Republican's move to purge the government of Soviet spies and possible Communist party members, and she enjoyed the damage it did to President Harry Truman's Democratic administration. But over time, McCarthy's witch-hunting tactics and his lack of concrete evidence to support his increasingly wild assertions made Smith uncomfortable. Reputations were trampled; careers were ruined without recourse to court proceedings.

At a speech in February 1950, Joseph McCarthy had waved a piece of paper, claiming it contained the names of 205 State Department employees whom the secretary of state knew were Communist Party members, yet whom still held their security-sensitive jobs. When Margaret Chase Smith pressed McCarthy to divulge the list, however, he evaded her and

Margaret Chase Smith, 1964 Courtesy Margaret Chase Smith Library, Skowhegan, Maine

did not produce any other solid proof of his claims. Although some senators, even those in his own party, privately questioned McCarthy's methods and his increasing power, they too were afraid of Soviet infiltration of the government—and they were afraid of Joe McCarthy's reprisals if they criticized him—so they remained silent. It was in this climate of fear, confused patriotism, and name-calling that Margaret Chase Smith stood up in the Senate chambers that June day in 1950.

> *Those of us who shout the loudest about Americanism in making character assassinations are all too frequently those who, by our own words and acts, ignore some of the basic principles of Americanism—*
> *The right to criticize;*
> *The right to hold unpopular beliefs;*
> *The right to protest;*
> *The right of independent thought;*
> *The exercise of these rights should not cost one single American citizen his reputation or his right to a livelihood nor should he be in danger of losing his reputation or livelihood merely because he happens to know someone who holds unpopular beliefs. Who of us doesn't? Otherwise none of us could call our souls our own. Otherwise thought control would have set in. . . .*

It was only a fifteen-minute speech, delivered in such a soft voice that some senators, once they realized the subject, had to lean forward in their seats to hear it. Margaret never mentioned Joe McCarthy by name, but her intention was clear. At the conclusion of her remarks, her aide, Bill Lewis, handed out two hundred mimeographed copies of her "Declaration of Conscience," which six other senators had secretly signed. Margaret's personal and political bravery that June day, her moral authority, independent nature, and refusal to be bullied into silence, catapulted her onto the national stage, where she would become one of the most influential women in American politics.

Margaret Chase was born on December 14, 1897, in the central Maine town of Skowhegan. Her parents, Carrie Murray and George Chase, christened her Marguerite Mandeline Chase at the local Notre Dame de Lourdes Catholic Church. Ancestors on her father's side were Puritan settlers of Massachusetts, who'd come to the frontier of Maine in the late 1700s to escape the political and religious control Boston exerted on its citizens. (Maine was part of Massachusetts until the 1820 Missouri Compromise.) On her mother's side, Margaret had Franco-American forebears, who had migrated south from Quebec, Canada. For a long time, such French-speaking ancestry was considered by some in Maine to be both a stigma and a political liability. Margaret was largely ignorant of that rich heritage until later in her life, when she embraced it.

During Margaret's childhood, Skowhegan was a small rural town of about five thousand, set on the banks of the Kennebec River, which powered shoe and wood-products factories. George Chase was one of the town's barbers. Until her marriage to George, Carrie Chase had worked at the shoe factory as a fancy stitcher, a highly skilled position. Because George suffered from terrible migraine headaches, he sometimes could not work, so to help the growing family survive, Carrie clerked part-time at the local five-and-dime. Margaret, as the eldest of six children, was her mother's partner in caring for the house and her younger brothers and sisters: three boys and two girls, born over a fifteen-year span. Of her parents Margaret later noted, "My father was a good father, but my mother was a wonderful mother."

School did not particularly interest Margaret, but the world of business did. While still very young, she asked for a job at the dime store where her mother sometimes worked. The owner jokingly told her she was too short and advised her to come back when she could reach the candy on the top shelf. Margaret took him seriously, and when she could reach the shelf at age thirteen, he hired her to clerk there after school.

At Skowhegan High School, Margaret was so disgusted with studying Latin and history that in her junior year she chose to move from the academic track of courses, geared to students who planned to attend college, to the commercial track. She played on her school's girls' basketball team, which won the state championship in 1916. Nicknamed "Marcus" by her teammates, Margaret loved the game, the camaraderie, and the competition. At only five feet three inches, she appeared taller because of her erect posture. "She walks as if she were stirring lemonade within herself," a classmate commented in their high school yearbook.

In the business world, from early on, Margaret was tireless and ambitious, always looking for better pay and job advancement. This led her, at sixteen, to become a substitute night telephone operator, work she credited with improving her memory as well as keeping her up-to-date on town affairs. At the time, all calls traveled through a central switchboard. Someone would call the operator and ask to be connected to a particular person, using the name rather than a number. Margaret memorized the numbers and often listened in on conversations.

One of the people in town she came to know through her telephone company job was Clyde Smith, the First Selectman in Skowhegan, who, at age twenty-nine, had been elected its youngest sheriff. When Margaret sat on night switchboard duty, he'd call to ask her for the time and weather. When she was seventeen and still a high school student, Clyde offered her a better-paying job as his part-time assistant in recording tax information, and he arranged for her to take typing and shorthand classes at night. Clyde was handsome and divorced, a ladies' man, a seasoned politician, and twenty-one years older than Margaret. From the beginning, their relationship—whatever it may have been—caused Skowhegan to talk. In any case, they worked well together and enjoyed a mutual attraction.

After she graduated from high school, Margaret went right into full-time work. Her family didn't have the money to pay for college, and she was eager to make her own way. When the full-time telephone operator job she wanted didn't materialize, she spent half a year teaching at a rural school. During that time, she felt very lonely and isolated from family and friends. She also was not particularly fond of working with rowdy children. The moment the telephone company job opened up, she grabbed it and moved back to her family's house on North Street, where she lived for thirteen more years.

The 1920s were a lively time for young working women, and Margaret took full advantage. She continued to see Clyde Smith, which fueled perpetual gossip, but she also traveled with a wide circle of friends. She belonged to a number of women's clubs, which were popular at the time and founded for recreation, self-improvement, and solidarity. In 1922, when she was twenty-five, she helped organize a local branch of the Business and Professional Women's Club, for which she served as vice president. She was elected its president in 1923. Public speaking—never something she did easily, nor did most other women, she felt—was one of the group's goals: "to get the girls to be able to stand up on their feet and say something," as she described it. In 1925, when Margaret was only twenty-seven, she became president of the club's state federation.

By this time, Margaret was in charge of circulation for Skowhegan's weekly *Independent-Reporter* newspaper, with a salary of $18 a week. During her years at the paper, the *Independent-Reporter* received an award for the largest circulation of any weekly in New England. Margaret was a go-getter, friendly, genial, patient, and very hard-working. While she considered herself "a girl about town" and a "semi-flapper" who cut her hair short and liked a good party, she never drank or smoked, and in fact often preferred to work and advance herself rather than attend purely social events. In her fine biography entitled *Margaret Chase Smith: Beyond Convention*, Patricia L. Smith describes Margaret, with her high cheekbones and strong jaw, as resembling "a ship's figure-head in proud profile."

In 1928, Margaret changed jobs again, becoming the office manager at Willard Cummings's woolen mill in Skowhegan. She'd heard about the opening when Cummings himself came into the newspaper office to place an ad, and she'd boldly asked, "What about me?" Working for Cummings, she earned $50 a week, a fortune in Skowhegan's economy, especially for a woman. Although she felt overwhelmed by what was demanded of her and claimed she "went home and cried every night for six months," she was determined to master the job and did.

One of Margaret's tasks was to do payroll and hand out checks to workers in the dye house and carbonizer room. Contrasting the pit-tance they received with Willard Cummings's vast wealth, she came to appreciate the plight of ordinary mill workers, who spent long hours in unhealthy surroundings, earning 26 to 28 cents an hour.

On May 14, 1930, at the beginning of the Great Depression, Margaret and Clyde Smith were married. She was thirty-two, he was fifty-three. In spite of Clyde's wish not to have two politicians in the family, Margaret ran for committeewoman from Skowhegan and won. In 1932, she gave up her job at the woolen mill and devoted the rest of her life to politics.

When Clyde was elected to the United States House of Representa-tives in 1936, the Smiths moved to Washington, where Margaret again asserted her independent nature. Instead of acting the part of decorative political wife, she insisted on managing Clyde's office and being paid for it. When he objected, she appealed to voters back in Maine, who signed a petition stating they'd as much voted for her as for him, and she carried the day. Because Clyde had already used up the allowance Congress gave him for paid staff, he paid Margaret $3,000 a year directly out of his own salary. In addition to being her husband's secretary, she also researched material for his proposals and speeches.

Although married now, Clyde did not change his ways. Margaret apparently learned about his infidelities early in their marriage; she never spoke of them, however, and did not leave him. The two continued to be an inseparable political team.

Less than a year after his term in the House started, Clyde suffered a heart attack, but Margaret kept his office running smoothly while he recovered. In spite of concerns about his health, Clyde ran for and won a second term. In 1940, Clyde's health was so poor that Margaret ran in the primary in his place—expecting to withdraw when he regained his strength. But Clyde did not recover. After his death, Margaret found herself heir to the Republican nomination and won the election that November.

During the difficult and lonely months that followed, Margaret threw herself into the tasks of a new House member. She made herself known for her work ethic and perfect attendance at all committee meetings and House sessions—not just for her trademark white gloves and hat, which newspapers never failed to mention. But something else made Margaret stand out: her principled independence. Often, she opposed the positions of Republican Party leaders, which earned her strong criticism. Her loyalty, however, went unwaveringly to Maine people and their interests.

While serving in the House, Margaret also became increasingly involved in military affairs, serving on what would become the Armed Services Committee. She visited soldiers and sailors stationed around the world and championed equal pay, equal rank, and equal retirement benefits for women in the military. She also helped found the WAVES (Women Accepted for Voluntary Emergency Service) and the Army-Navy Permanent Nurses Corp.

Back home, Margaret was a popular politician and vote-getter. In 1948, she entered the Republican primary for one of Maine's Senate seats, campaigning against Horace Hildreth, the incumbent governor, as well as two other powerful candidates. Against the odds, she won the nomination, though the Republican Party refused to back her in the general election. She didn't need the party's help, it turned out. Her low-budget, grassroots campaign was so successful that she earned 70 percent of the vote. She made history by becoming the first woman to serve in both houses of Congress and the first elected to the Senate in her own right.

At Margaret's side, in the roles of administrative assistant, campaigner, and life partner, was her aide, William E. Lewis Jr. Fifteen years younger than Margaret, Bill was a Navy man who devoted himself to her career, much as she had devoted herself to her husband Clyde's.

As a freshman senator, and the only woman among ninety-five men in the "most exclusive men's club in the world," Margaret did her homework and sought important committee appointments but generally kept her mouth shut until—in spite of political expediency—she decided that "something [had] to be done about that man," Joseph McCarthy.

After her "Declaration of Conscience" speech, which she wrote with Bill Lewis, the entire country knew about Margaret Chase Smith. Controversy raged. Many applauded her courage and willingness to challenge McCarthy's reign of terror. Most analysts agreed that she was morally right but politically wrong. "I wouldn't want to say anything that bad about the Republican Party," wryly noted Democratic President Harry S. Truman the day Margaret delivered her speech. The next day, in a newspaper column, Bernard M. Baruch wrote, "If a man had made the Declaration of Conscience, he would be the next President of the United States."

Less than a month after Margaret's speech, however, on June 25, 1950, North Korea invaded South Korea, and the United States again went to war, further stirring anti-Communist sentiment around the country. It would be four more years before the Senate officially censured Joseph McCarthy, but Margaret's "Declaration of Conscience" speech marked the beginning of the end for McCarthyism. In the meantime,

McCarthy himself set out to punish Margaret. First, he kicked her off the Investigations Subcommittee, an influential post, and saw to it that she was removed from the Republican Policy Committee. But she never backed down and never stopped speaking her mind. In spite of her clash with McCarthy, she managed to become a member of two important Senate committees: Appropriations and Armed Services.

Three more times she won reelection to the Senate—in 1954, 1960, and 1966—each time by a 70 percent plurality. If in Washington Margaret struggled with members of her own political party, her Maine constituents—Republican, Democrat, and Independent—loved her. Citizens in other parts of the country too, it seemed, responded enthusiastically to her plainspoken, honest, sometimes hard-nosed, ethical stands. By this time, Margaret was used to breaking new political ground for her gender, but in January of 1964, she did something that would have been unthinkable even a few years before: She announced her candidacy for President of the United States. Six months later, at the Cow Palace in San Francisco, she became the first woman to have her name placed in nomination for US President at a convention of a major political party. She didn't win the nomination—Barry Goldwater did—but she made a lasting impression on American politics.

After serving in the US Senate for twenty-four years, Margaret finally lost a reelection bid in 1973. Although she retired from elected office at the age of seventy-six, she did not retire from public life. At her home overlooking the Kennebec River in Skowhegan, she began to plan for the Margaret Chase Smith Library, which opened in 1982. There she met with visitors, researchers, policymakers, and schoolchildren. She also lectured widely at colleges around the country, conducted public policy seminars, and wrote for newspapers and magazines. In addition she published two books: *Gallant Women*, a collection of biographies of American women, and *Declaration of Conscience*, which dealt with the workings of American government.

During her lifetime she received ninety-five honorary degrees, and in 1973 she became one of the original inductees to the National Women's Hall of Fame. The Associated Press named her Woman of the Year in 1948, 1949, 1950, and 1957. Although she never called herself a feminist, her life exemplified equality and paved the way for countless women, not only from Maine but from around the world.

In 1995, Margaret suffered a stroke, then caught pneumonia. She died at home on Memorial Day that year. She was ninety-seven years old. Her own words—unadorned and rich with Maine understatement—might serve as a fitting motto for her extraordinary life: "When people keep telling you that you can't do a thing, you kind of like to try it."

MARGUERITE YOURCENAR

———•◦•———

(1903–1987)

*The "Immortal" of
Mount Desert Island*

In France, Marguerite Yourcenar is celebrated as one of the twentieth century's most brilliant writers—historical novelist, intellectual, essayist, poet, translator. In Maine, by contrast, her name usually draws a blank. And yet for almost forty years she chose to live not in Paris but in Northeast Harbor, a small village on Mount Desert Island, off the Maine coast. Here, few locals read her books or had any inkling of how famous she was. They referred to her simply as "Madame," which suited her to a T.

Mount Desert, home to Acadia National Park, was named by the French explorer Samuel de Champlain as he sailed past in 1604. In his journal, noting the treeless expanse of what is now Cadillac Mountain, he called the island "Isle des Mont-Déserts"—Island of Bare Mountains. Marguerite Yourcenar and Grace Frick, her American companion and translator, spent eight summers there in the 1940s. Its beauty captivated them. They loved its rounded pink granite mountains, its forests of spruce and pine, its blue and green and sun-gold views of Penobscot Bay. They were drawn, too, by the bracing isolation of inhabiting North America's very edge.

For several summers they looked for a house to buy. It couldn't be expensive, and it had to be within walking distance of a post office.

Marguerite Yourcenar Courtesy Petite Plaisance Trust

(They didn't own a car—and never would—preferring to rent one if necessary.) In September of 1950, they finally found their place. It felt like an epiphany. The white clapboard Cape on an acre of land looked humble compared to the grand mansions on the ocean side of South Shore Road, but it had enough land to plant vegetable and flower gardens, and it backed up to a stretch of woods. It seemed "a place of tranquility and possible abandon," as Marguerite described it. They called their new home Petite Plaisance—Little Pleasure.

Marguerite Antoinette Jeanne Marie Ghislaine Cleenewerck de Crayencour was born on June 8, 1903, in Brussels, Belgium. Her mother, Fernande, was Belgian; her father, Michel de Cleenewerck de Crayencour, a French aristocrat of Flemish descent. Fernande died of puerperal fever ten days after Marguerite's birth. Cared for by house-maids and adored by her father, she claimed never to have missed having a mother. She and Michel spent long happy summers at Mont-Noir, the family's château near the Belgian border, where she roamed the grounds freely. "In my childhood, people were not very important," she once said. "I grew up with nature and animals"—lambs, dogs, ponies, a don-key to ride. To please her, Michel even had the horns of a goat painted gold. During the winters, they lived in Lille or on the Riviera, where he devoted himself to leisure pursuits, especially gambling.

Marguerite was a precocious child. She had no formal schooling but learned to read at a young age, inspired by her father to explore the four thousand books in Mont-Noir's oak-paneled library. At eight, she read *Phaedra*, a play in verse by the seventeenth-century French playwright Racine. She was also gifted with languages. Her father taught her Latin at ten and Greek at twelve. On her own, she learned Italian, a little Ger-man and Spanish, and later some Japanese.

Michel encouraged his daughter's writing, and she grew up confi-dent in her own bright literary future. When she was sixteen, he paid to publish her first book of poetry. One evening, the two of them made up the nom de plume "Yourcenar," an acronym of "Crayencour," which she eventually adopted as her legal name, being, as she said, "very fond of the letter Y."

Michel sold Mont-Noir when Marguerite was nine, and they moved to Paris. While he gambled away large sums of money, she explored the city, visiting museums and bookstalls and alleyways paved with cobbles.

During World War I, they fled France to live in England, where Michel "taught" her English by having her read out loud from a bilingual English-Greek edition of *The Meditations of Marcus Aurelius*. Although she later spoke and read English very well, she never lost her strong French accent. (In Northeast Harbor, locals would say, "Madame speaks the same as she writes books.")

After the war, Marguerite and her father eventually settled in Monte Carlo. Bankrupt from gambling debts, he died in Lausanne, Switzerland, in 1929, just before her first novel, *Alexis*, was published. She cried then quickly forgot him, she told an interviewer for a 1981 *New York Times Magazine* profile. "Years later I began thinking about him; I had to learn to know him over again. I realize now that he was the first great friend I ever had."

For the next decade, thanks to a legacy from her mother, Marguerite traveled throughout Europe, especially in Greece. She was avid for adventure—having affairs with both men and women, and writing, always writing. During that time she fell in love with her French editor at Grasset, André Fraigneau. He didn't reciprocate—he was homosexual—but admired her artistry so much that he published several of her books, including *Denier du Rêve* (*A Coin in Nine Hands*) and a long prose poem, *Feux* (*Fires*).

In her early twenties, Marguerite's passion for ancient Greece and Rome embodied itself in the historical figure of Emperor Hadrian, who ruled the Roman Empire from AD 117 to 138. She visited places he'd visited and read what he'd read, drinking up his world like a thirsty plant. For Marguerite, Hadrian was a man of intriguing contrasts: a soldier who matured into a masterful statesman and advocate of peace; a contemplative student of human nature, including his own, who in midlife loved a beautiful Greek boy, Antinous. She completed two entire drafts of her Hadrian novel only to abandon the project, believing it a failure.

In 1937, Marguerite met Grace Frick (whom she called by both names) in the Parisian hotel where the women were staying. An English professor, raised in Kansas City, Grace was Marguerite's age-mate, bright, well-read, and bold. When she returned to the United States to begin work on her PhD thesis at Yale, she invited Marguerite to join her. They lived together in New Haven that winter. They made a striking couple. Marguerite—short, handsome, and heavyset—had intense blue eyes and a regal air; Grace was tall, slim, and athletic, bursting with energy and fun. Yourcenar's dreamy temperament contrasted with Grace's more practical and outgoing nature. Somehow, it worked. They would live together as a couple for forty years.

Their future was by no means established, however, when Marguerite visited Grace again in October of 1939. The ship she boarded would be the last one to leave Bordeaux, France, before World War II broke out and France fell to the Germans. To evade enemy submarines, the ship zigzagged across the Atlantic to New York. Marguerite couldn't imagine returning to a Nazi-occupied France. Besides, the money from her legacy had run out, and so she stayed in America.

Months stretched into years, during which the two shared an apartment in Hartford, Connecticut. While Grace ran Hartford Junior College, Marguerite made the long commute by bus and train to Bronxville, New York, to teach French and comparative literature at Sarah Lawrence College. During this time, she was attracted to the beauty and cadence of Negro spirituals, some of which she translated into French.

But for Marguerite, the war years were deeply troubling. She seemed adrift, for all she and Grace enjoyed their summer visits to Mount Desert. A lifelong pacifist, she mourned the devastation of two world wars, their terrible cost to life, environment, and culture. Also, she was a literary unknown in America, since none of her four novels had been published in English. But that loss of identity paled against what felt like a painful creative death: Her own wellspring of writing had dried up.

Then, in 1948, several trunks she'd stored in Switzerland before the war finally found their way to Hartford. Most of the contents she gladly burned. But at the bottom of one trunk lay something remarkable—a few pages of another Hadrian draft she'd forgotten about completely. It was the beginnings of a letter, written in the voice of Hadrian himself near the end of his life, addressed to his adopted grandson and heir, Marcus Aurelius. Here was the way forward. Let Hadrian tell his own story.

For two years she worked feverishly, joyfully. She was older now, more knowledgeable about Hadrian's life and cultural context. And hardship had tempered her enough so that she could truly inhabit the soul of the sixty-two-year-old emperor who lay dying. While she was writing the book, she and Grace moved into Petite Plaisance, an old farmhouse with few amenities. Through sawing, plastering, and hammering, along with a furnace to install and a kitchen and bathroom to equip, Marguerite kept working.

On the night of December 26, 1950, she wrote the book's ending, Hadrian's death, which happened in the year 138 at Baiae, a seaside resort on the Bay of Naples. Inside the intimacy of her thoughts it was a sweltering July day, while on Mount Desert it had been dark since 4:00 p.m. and bitter cold. "At the time," she later said, "a half-dozen workers were painting and doing repairs in the next room, and every now and then I stopped my writing to chat with them."

Though Marguerite could lose herself in worlds of her own creation, she would willingly interrupt her writing trance to talk with a workman or visitor, moving seamlessly from an imaginary world to a clamorous, banging one. But it makes sense when explained by the American Yourcenar scholar Joan E. Howard, who first met Marguerite in 1982 when writing her PhD thesis on the author's novels and plays. "Images were central to Madame Yourcenar's creative process," notes Howard. "She sometimes said it was like watching a film in her mind's eye." Most of these images had appeared to her in her early twenties. It would take a lifetime to translate them onto the page.

A year after its completion, *Mémoires d'Hadrien* was published in France. Marguerite was forty-eight years old. She assumed the book would attract fewer than a dozen readers because it dealt with philosophical and historical subjects not in fashion at the time. No one was more surprised than she when it was immediately embraced both as a masterpiece and a best seller.

Grace Frick translated the book, with Yourcenar's collaboration, in the studio where its last chapters were written. To better consult about a word, a phrase, a nuance, the women sat facing each other at a wide table, behind portable manual typewriters—their pattern for the next thirty years. In 1954, Farrar, Straus and Giroux published *Memoirs of Hadrian* in the United States, where it also, perhaps more surprisingly, became a bestseller.

Hadrian's success brought both riches and fame. It also brought sharp scrutiny from the author's writing peers in France. What possibly could Madame Yourcenar be thinking to live as a "recluse" in the wilds of America? Why wouldn't she return to France, closer to her culture and language? She had *even* become an American citizen!

But Marguerite had no interest in joining literary circles and no patience for squabbling critics. She kept up a lively correspondence with writers she admired, and that was enough. Should one of her books require explaining, she'd do it best herself. Also, if she lived on the coast of Brittany—the closest French equivalent to Maine's rocky shores—interviewers and autograph seekers would no doubt besiege the place, sapping both her energy and her time.

Joan Howard, who knew Madame Yourcenar well in the 1980s, was struck by her warmth, her sincere interest in others, the pleasure she took in good conversation. She was hardly a "recluse." Her friends came from all walks of Mount Desert life—from island fishermen to the local librarian, from the woman who cleaned her house to wealthy summer people in the mansions of Seal Harbor. Caring little for self-promotion, she preferred learning the details of other people's lives—what a lobsterman used to bait his traps, how a carpenter solved a construction problem. She loved outings of every kind, whether taking her dog to the vet on the mainland or shopping for groceries in Bar Harbor or enjoying tea and popovers at the Jordan Pond House. She was not the kind of intellectual who ever lost touch with the simple joys of everyday life.

At Petite Plaisance, afternoon tea was a ritual in the back garden on fine days or in the parlor in front of the fireplace on cool, rainy ones. Between 4:30 and 5:00, other activities stopped. Marguerite made her own blend of Lapsang Souchong and Earl Grey teas and served Pepperidge Farm cookies. In their early days, she and Grace had an open house on Sunday afternoons for which she baked pastries, and Grace made drinks. At New Year's they served spiked eggnog with plenty of spike. They often invited local children to Petite Plaisance to celebrate holidays from different parts of the world.

Because Grace was an avid equestrian, Marguerite signed up for lessons at a local stable on the condition that her young teacher speak French. A bit tentative on horseback, Marguerite was nevertheless a good sport. She would later say that some of her loveliest experiences of nature took place while in the saddle.

For six months of the year, winter into spring, the women left Northeast Harbor and traveled the world. They spent weeks exploring Hadrian's Wall in the north of England and frequented village pubs. The two fell in love with Scandinavia. Yourcenar didn't like to fly, so they always went by ship. Not light packers, they once returned home with two dozen suitcases and trunks. Monsieur, the first of three beloved cocker spaniels, also traveled with them. Monsieur and his successor, Valentine, even visited museums in Europe.

While Marguerite enjoyed the pageantry and ritual of her Catholic upbringing—religious parades at Mont-Noir, the waving of incense, the chanting in Latin—she called the world's major religions, Judaism, Christianity, and Islam, "the three great imposters" for the violence perpetrated in their names. She herself was drawn to Buddhism, which she studied in depth. It spoke to her sense of being part of a universal whole. She felt an intimate connection with the world that extended to animals, oceans, rocks, and trees. Ordinary objects transformed into extraordinary ones, stuff of the spirit as well as of the material world. In the kitchen at Petite Plaisance, as Joan Howard recalled, Madame once stopped to touch the edge of the sturdy pine table, as if truly communing with its essence. *"Le bon bois de la table,"* she said. The good wood of the table. This ability to profoundly experience sights and smells and sounds saturates her writing and makes it glow. Readers, too, are mesmerized.

Marguerite's major project during the 1960s was her novel *L'Œuvre au Noir*, whose evocation of conflict in sixteenth-century Europe echoes a decade of upheaval in America. Marguerite and Grace both actively opposed the Vietnam War, participating in protest rallies on the island and writing letters to political leaders. To inspire friends and neighbors to join in the fight, they played protest songs by Woody Guthrie and Pete Seeger at their Sunday open houses. They were also active on behalf of civil rights. Yourcenar took the plight of US blacks seriously, publishing a sixty-page historical essay on the experience of African Americans. Any group advocating for justice, for animal and human rights or thoughtful stewardship of the planet, Marguerite supported.

For her entire life she resisted what she considered the divisiveness of labels, from racism to nationalism to chauvinism of any kind. Though she lived with a woman for forty years, she didn't call herself a lesbian. Neither did she think of herself as a feminist. Raised in privilege, she had difficulty accepting the degree to which other women struggled.

L'Œuvre au Noir was published in France in 1968 to instant critical and popular acclaim, winning the Prix Femina that year by a unanimous vote. The book takes place during the sixteenth century, a tumultuous, violent time when old ways clashed with the new thinking of the Reformation and Renaissance. The story traces the life and death of Zeno, the illegitimate son of a rich banking family in Bruges, Belgium. Physician, philosopher, alchemist, and scientist, he opposes the status quo in all realms, dedicating his life, instead, to a search for what is true. He was Yourcenar's favorite of her characters. *L'Œuvre au Noir*'s publication coincided with the student uprisings of May 1968 at universities in France and the United States. Zeno struck a chord, as if directly speaking for young protestors who rallied against the war as well as against hate, hypocrisy, and greed.

Pleased at the reception *L'Œuvre au Noir* was receiving, Marguerite and Grace enjoyed touring England, France, and Belgium. Three years later, however, their travels together stopped. Cancer, which Grace had battled since a mastectomy in 1958, was spreading throughout her body. For eight years, they stayed at Petite Plaisance year-round as Grace weakened and her pain grew unbearable. It was a terrible time. Marguerite nursed her and worked on what she conceived of as a family trilogy called *Le Labyrinthe du Monde*. In spite of her declining health, Grace struggled ever harder to translate *L'Œuvre au Noir* into English. In 1976, it was finally published in America as *The Abyss* and drew high praise. "If reading 'Hadrian' is like gazing on white marble," wrote Joan Acocella in a *New Yorker* piece, "reading *The Abyss* is like breaking open a clod of earth and finding strange, dark things: glints and bones and bugs, slimes and rots, sulfur and verdigris."

Grace died in 1979. She'd been Marguerite's friend, lover, companion, and translator—her family. She'd also served as a faithful guardian who'd created the structure in which Marguerite's writing flourished.

Grace had given another gift too: her unique, quirky, and freewheeling self. She was buried in the Brookside Cemetery in Somesville, across the sound from Northeast Harbor.

Grace's illness and slow dying had taken its toll on Marguerite. As much as she grieved this loss, however, it was also a relief. Grace's suffering—and her own—had ended. She was now free to travel again, something she had greatly missed. This she did in the company of a young American photographer named Jerry Wilson, who'd come to Petite Plaisance in the late 1970s as the director's assistant on a French television documentary. Theirs was a volatile relationship, defying labels—she in her late seventies, he in his early thirties and gay.

As Marguerite's fame and stature grew, Jean d'Ormesson, the former editor of the French newspaper *Le Figaro*, asked if he might nominate her for admission to the Académie Française. Election to the academy, which was founded by Cardinal Richelieu in 1635, still stands as the highest accolade in all of French letters. The Académie Française has only forty members, who select a new member only after one of them dies. "The Immortals," as they are called, are charged with creating the official dictionary of the French language. Marguerite had forged her own life's mission to write and never sought the validation of such recognition, but she told d'Ormesson that, if chosen, she would at least not refuse the honor.

While no one disputed the beauty and power of Marguerite Yourcenar's writing, the depth of her historical scholarship, or the brilliance of her mind, there were other problems. Customarily, potential members to the Académie Française lobbied heavily for admission, which she wouldn't do. And she was a woman. None had ever been elected in the academy's 350 years. No specific rules forbade it, but precedent seemed to indicate, "It's simply not done." Furthermore, she wasn't even a citizen of France nor had she lived there for some forty years. All of this caused a furor.

Marguerite herself was more interested in bird-watching than award-garnering. During the spring of 1980, while the storm raged over her nomination, she and Jerry Wilson planned a Caribbean cruise. Her election was announced as the boat set sail. The trouble over nationality was quickly smoothed over when the French government granted Marguerite dual citizenship.

The induction ceremony, filled with centuries-old pomp and tradition, took place in Paris in late January of 1981. Instead of the uniform the male Immortals wore—long-tailed Napoleonic waistcoats embroidered with olive tree leaves and black-feathered bicorne hats—Madame wore evening clothes designed by an admirer, fashion icon Yves Saint Laurent. Refusing the ceremonial sword, she agreed to accept a gold coin from the reign of Hadrian. In the academy's long history, it has had a total of 726 members. Marguerite has since been joined by seven other women *Immortelles*.

France's then-president, Valéry Giscard d'Estaing, who attended Yourcenar's induction with his wife, invited Madame to have dinner with him at the Elysée Palace, the official residence. Not sharing his political views, she turned him down. But a year later she accepted when Giscard d'Estaing's left-wing successor, François Mitterrand, extended a similar invitation.

While Petite Plaisance was still home, Yourcenar and Jerry Wilson traveled most of the year, visiting Kenya, Japan, India, and Europe. She was a celebrity, sought after all over the world. But now she took planes and left her portable typewriter at home in favor of a journal and pen.

Marguerite's great love of nature, as well as her passion for human and animal rights, endured. Late in her life she was a contributing member to sixty-some organizations—from Greenpeace to Planned Parenthood to the World Wildlife Federation, from antinuclear nonprofits to one that looked after the horses of Cairo, Egypt, when they could no longer pull carriages. She became friends with French actress Brigitte

Bardot, a fellow animal rights activist. Marguerite's letter to the Parisian newspaper *Le Monde*, which drew attention to the plight of baby seals, galvanized an international response.

In 1986, Jerry died of complications from AIDS. His death weighed heavily on Marguerite, as did a growing sense of her own mortality. She was eighty-two. Still, Petite Plaisance offered up its tranquil solace, and she was able to keep working there, retaining her intellectual if not her physical vigor. She continued writing her long family memoir and translated two works into French: James Baldwin's *The Amen Corner* in 1983 and Yukio Mishimia's *Five Modern No Plays* (from Japanese) in 1984. She also wrote an essay about the Argentine writer Jorge Luis Borges.

Marguerite had packed for one last trip to Europe when she had a massive stroke and was taken to Mount Desert Hospital. On December 17, 1987, at the age of eighty-four, she died. More than once, she'd said that death didn't frighten her, that she hoped to die, as her character Hadrian expressed it, "with open eyes." At her wish, she was buried next to Grace Frick at Brookside Cemetery.

In her will, Marguerite Yourcenar left Petite Plaisance to remain exactly as she had loved it in her lifetime. Joan Howard, a member of the Petite Plaisance Trust, is also the director of the house museum. Thirty years after Madame's death, Joan continues to lead tours by appointment from mid-June through August.

We wait outside, six pilgrims. We have admired the white picket fence, the wide lawn, the kiwi vine that's swallowing the front porch, and talked to the gardener, who also knew Madame. She tells us it's a spring garden really, full of trillium and lily-of-the-valley at the right season.

Now it's early August, and the peony tree has finished blooming. The bee balm is out, and herbs and vegetables are coming along, the ones Marguerite herself grew: cucumber, parsley, basil, lettuce, tomatoes. Pole beans, climbing a teepee of sticks, have begun producing pods. We take the woods' path, rich with moss, to the gravestones of Marguerite's four dogs: Monsieur, Valentine, Zoe, and Fou-Kou, whose name means "happiness" in Japanese.

Inside, the eight small rooms are filled floor to ceiling with books: seven thousand of them, shelved chronologically from earliest antiquity in the author's studio to twentieth-century fiction in Madame's bedroom. The rooms, with their Piranesi prints and knickknacks and photos and shawl-draped chairs, feel comfy and intimate. And they hum with her presence. She's there, working at her table, across from Grace. She's in the rustic kitchen too, where she liked to do the cooking. Simple fare, nothing gourmet, just good fresh ingredients from the garden, chopped on a butcher block that still sits in the middle of the room. It was used for fruits and vegetables, not meat; in the words of her character Zeno, she did not like to "digest agonies."

Perhaps in honor of her Belgian ancestors, Madame liked a glass of beer at lunch, Joan tells us—at dinner a small cup of wine. We notice the aluminum pots and pans hanging at the ready from hooks along a wall. We marvel at the *bon bois de la table*, warm to the touch. On two kitchen shelves sit gallon glass jars on which she painted French names: *pâtes* (pasta), *biscottes* (crackers), *abricots* (apricots). When asked, "Isn't the word 'corn-flakes' English?" Joan laughs. "They say the hyphen makes it French."

It's hard to leave Petite Plaisance. But Madame has left behind not just a welcoming place but a luminous body of work, enough for decades of reading and rereading. Hers was a fascinating journey, full of purpose and meaning. World traveler, French classicist, she could have lived anywhere but chose Maine as her anchor.

When French journalist Matthieu Galey asked Madame why she thought readers considered her a wise advisor, one who could "teach them how to live," she answered this way:

My primary purpose has always been to discover how I might live a better life, how I might live the best life I am capable of. My books have been a series of explorations paralleling my personal explorations. People are likely to ask directions of someone they meet along a road somewhere, to find out about where he's coming from and where he thinks he's going.

BIBLIOGRAPHY

Marguerite-Blanche Thibodeau Cyr

Acadian & French Canadian Ancestral Home. "Kamouraska History." www.acadian
-home.org/kamouraskaenglish.html.

Acadian Genealogy Homepage. "'Tante Blanche' was heroine of Colonists' black
famine." www.acadian.org/blanche.html.

Albert, Thomas. *The History of Madawaska*. Madawaska, ME: Madawaska Historical
Society, 1989.

Chassé, Geraldine. Interview by author, Madawaska, Maine, June 18, 2004.

Franco-American Women's Institute. "Tante Blanche Museum, Madawaska, Maine."
www.fawi.net/tanteblanche.html.

Kate Furbish

Agger, Lee. *Women of Maine*. Portland, ME: Guy Gannett Publishing, 1982.

Bonta, Marcia Meyers. *Women in the Field: America's Pioneering Women Naturalists*.
College Station: Texas A&M University Press, 1991.

Furbish, Kate. Kate Furbish Collection. George J. Mitchell Department of Special
Collections & Archives, Bowdoin College Library, Brunswick, Maine.

Graham, Ada, and Frank Graham Jr. *Kate Furbish and the Flora of Maine*. Gardiner,
ME: Tilbury House, 1995.

James, Edward T., ed. *Notable American Women 1607–1950: A Biographical
Dictionary*. Vol. 1, A–F. Cambridge, MA: Belknap Press of Harvard University
Press.

Abbie Burgess Grant

Clifford, Mary Louise, and J. Candace. *Women Who Kept the Lights: An
Illustrated History of Female Lighthouse Keepers*. Williamsburg, VA: Cypress
Communications, 1993.

Maine: An Encyclopedia. "Abbie Burgess Grant." http://maineanencyclopedia.com/
grant-abbie-burgess.

New England Lighthouses. "Matinicus Rock Lighthouse." http://www.nelights.com/
exploring/Maine/matinicus_rock_light.html.

Parker, Gail Underwood. It Happened in Maine. Guilford, CT: Globe Pequot Press,
2004.

Sargent, Ruth Sexton, and Dorothy Holder Jones. The Original Biography of Abbie
Burgess, Lighthouse Heroine. Whiting, ME: Lighthouse Digest, 1998.

US Coast Guard. "USCGC Abbie Burgess (WLM 553)" http://www.uscg.mil/d1/ cgcabbieburgess.

Lillian M. N. Stevens

Agger, Lee. *Women of Maine*. Portland, ME: Guy Gannett Publishing, 1982.

Giele, Janet Zollinger. *Two Paths to Women's Equality: Temperance, Suffrage, and the Origins of Modern Feminism*. New York: Twayne Publishers, 1995.

Gordon, Anna A. *What Lillian M. N. Stevens Said*. Evanston, IL: National Woman's Christian Temperance Union, 1914.

Leavitt, Gertrude Stevens, and Margaret L. Sargent. *Lillian M. N. Stevens: A Life Sketch*. 1921.

"Mrs. L. M. N. Stevens Passes Away at Her Home." *Daily Eastern Argus* (Portland), April 7, 1914.

Portland Women's History Trail. Stroudwater District. "Home of Lillian Ames Stevens." http://media.usm.maine.edu/~pwht/places/stroudwater-district/sd05 -home-of-lillian-ames-stevens.html.

Ward, Sarah F. *Lillian M. N. Stevens: Champion of Justice*. Evanston, IL: Signal Press, 2004.

Sarah Orne Jewett

Blanchard, Paula. *Sarah Orne Jewett: Her World and Her Work*. Reading, MA: Addison-Wesley Publishing Company, 1994.

Dupre, Jeff, producer and director. *Out of the Past*. PBS documentary video, 1997.

Jewett, Sarah Orne. *The Country of the Pointed Firs and Other Stories*. Garden City, NY: Doubleday & Company, 1956.

———. "Looking Back on Girlhood." *The Youth's Companion* 65, no. 1 (January 7, 1892): 5–6.

Morrison, Jane. *Master Smart Woman*. Documentary film, 1985.

Morrison, Jane, Peter Namuth, and Cynthia Keyworth. *Master Smart Woman: A Portrait of Sarah Orne Jewett*. Unity, ME: North Country Press, 1988.

Silverthorne, Elizabeth. *Sarah Orne Jewett: A Writer's Life*. Woodstock, NY: Overlook Press, 1993.

Cornelia "Fly Rod" Crosby

Elden, Alfred, "Fly Rod, Now 83, Famous Writer of Outdoor Stories, Was Maine's First Publicity Agent." *Portland Sunday Telegram*, December 19, 1937.

Hunter, Julia A., and Earle G. Shettleworth Jr. *Fly Rod Crosby: The Woman Who Marketed Maine*. Gardiner, ME: Tilbury House Publishers, 2000.

McCubrey, March O. "Diana of the Maine Woods: An Analysis of Cornelia 'Fly Rod' Crosby's Involvement in Women's Outdoor Sporting Culture." MA thesis, Bowling Green State University, 1995.

Northeast Historic Film. "Home, the Story of Maine – The Nation's Playground." http://oldfilm.org/content/home-story-maine-nations-playground.

Verde, Thomas A. "First Lady of the Maine Woods." *Down East: The Magazine of Maine*, August 1998, 57–59.

Women's History Trail: Augusta, Maine. "Cornelia 'Fly Rod' Crosby." dll.umaine.edu/
historytrail/site6.html.

Lillian "La Nordica" Norton
Brockway, Wallace, and Herbert Weinstock. *The World of Opera*. New York: Pantheon,
1962.
Glackens, Ira. *Yankee Diva: Lillian Nordica and the Golden Days of Opera*. New York:
Coleridge Press, 1963.
Klein, Herman. *Great Women Singers of My Time*. London: G. Routledge & Co., 1931.
"Lillian Nordica: Opera singer who gained international fame." *Bangor Daily News*,
March 8, 2008. http://archive.bangordailynews.com/2008/03/08/lillian-nordica
-opera-singer-who-gained-international-fame.
Marston Records. "Three American Sopranos: Lillian Nordica, Olive Fremstad and
Ada Adini." www.marstonrecords.com/3_sopranos/3sopranos_ward.htm.
"Nordica Homestead Museum." *Maine Archives and Museums Newsletter* 3, no. 4
(November 2000): 7–8.
Suhm-Binder, Andrea. Andrea's cantabile-subito: A Site for Collectors of Great
Singers of the Past. "Nordica, Lillian." www.cantabile-subito.de/Sopranos/
Nordica_Lillian/nordica_lillian.htm.

Josephine Diebitsch Peary
Friends of Peary's Eagle Island. "About Peary." www.pearyeagleisland.org.
Hobbs, William Herbert. *Peary*. New York: Macmillan Company, 1936.
Letters: Josephine Diebitsch Peary to Robert F. Peary. March 1900 and April 3, 1900.
Josephine Diebitsch Peary Papers. University of New England, Maine Women
Writers Collection, Portland.
"Mrs. Peary Dead; Admiral's Widow." *New York Times*, December 20, 1955.
Peary, Josephine Diebitsch. *My Arctic Journal: A Year Among Ice-Fields and Eskimos*.
New York: Contemporary Publishing Co., 1893.
———. *The Snow Baby: A True Story with True Pictures*. New York: Frederick A.
Stokes, 1901.
Peary-MacMillan Arctic Museum. Biographies. "Josephine Diebitsch Peary." https://
www.bowdoin.edu/arctic-museum/biographies/jpeary.shtml.
Stafford, Edward Peary. "Introduction to My Arctic Journal." www.pearyhenson.org/
Myarcticjournal.
Tanguay, Corina. "Josephine Diebitsch Peary." Women and the American Experience.

Florence Nicolar Shay
Ghere, David L. "Assimilation, Termination, or Tribal Rejuvenation: Maine Indian
Affairs in the 1950s." *Maine Historical Quarterly* 24, no. 2 (Fall 1984): 239–64.
McBride, Bunny. "Princess Watahwaso: Bright Star of the Penobscot." In Marli F.
Weiner, *Of Place & Gender: Women in Maine History*. Orono: University of Maine
Press, 2005.
"Mr. and Mrs. Leo Shay Observe Golden Wedding Anniversary." *Bangor Daily News*,
January 27, 1958.

BIBLIOGRAPHY

Nicolar, Emma. Interview by author, Indian Island, Maine, December 3, 2004.

Nicolar, Joseph. *Life & Traditions of the Red Man*. Old Town, ME: Penobscot Nation Museum, 2002 (reprinted).

Rolde, Neil. *Unsettled Past, Unsettled Future: The Story of Maine Indians*. Gardiner, ME: Tilbury House Publishers, 2004.

Shay, Caron. Interview by author, Indian Island, Maine, December 3, 2004.

Shay, Charles N. Interview by author, Indian Island, Maine, December 3, 2004.

Shay, Florence Nicolar. *History of the Penobscot Tribe of Indians*. Old Town, ME: Florence Nicolar Shay, 1941.

Marguerite Zorach

Bourgeault, Cynthia. "'Very Much Her Own Person.'" *Down East: The Magazine of Maine*, August 1987, 66–71, 102–3.

Hoffman, Marilyn Friedman. *Marguerite and William Zorach: The Cubist Years: 1915–1918*. Hanover, NH: University Press of New England, 1987.

Ipcar, Dahlov. Interview by author, Georgetown, Maine, October 28, 2004.

Nicoll, Jessica, director of the Smith College Museum of Art; former chief curator, Portland Museum of Art. Interview by author, Portland, Maine, October 22, 2004.

Pierce, Kathleen. "Maine artist Dahlov Ipcar, 98, savors life, continues to paint." *Bangor Daily News*, November 18, 2015. http://bangordailynews.com/2015/11/18/living/maine-artist-dahlov-ipcar-98-savors-life-continues-to-paint.

Seligmann, Herbert J. "The Zorachs of Robinhood Cove." *Down East: The Magazine of Maine*, August 1958.

Tarbell, Roberta. *Marguerite Zorach: The Early Years, 1908–1920*. Exhibition catalogue. Washington, DC: National Collection of Fine Arts, Smithsonian Institution, 1974.

Zorach Collection. "Marguerite Zorach." www.zorachart.com/marguerite.html.

Zorach, Peggy. Interview by author, Georgetown, Maine, October 28, 2004.

Toy Len Goon

Album Dedicated to the Loving Memory of Toy Len Goon, 1994. Pamphlet 3165, spiral-bound. Collections of the Maine Historical Society, Portland, Maine.

Book of Memories: The Family of Dogan and Toy Len Goon, 2003. S.C. 1047. Collections of the Maine Historical Society, Portland, Maine.

Field, Jacqueline. "Mud Silk and the Chinese Laundress: From the South China Silk Industry to Mud Silk Suits in Maine." *Textile History* 45, no. 2 (November 2014): 234–60.

Guen, Leo T., and Amy Guen, grandson and daughter-in-law of Toy Len Goon. E-mail correspondence with author, September 9–19, 2015.

Hammond, Jonathan. "Anatomy of a Taishan Village." EDRA (Environmental Design Research Association) 21, 1990, 147–56. www.edra.org/sites/default/files/publications/EDRA21-Hammond-147-156.pdf.

Libby, Gary, historian of Chinese in Maine. Interview by author, Portland, Maine, June 16, 2015. E-mail correspondence with author, June 17–September 16, 2015.

Wong, Doris O., daughter of Toy Len Goon. Interview by author, Boston, July 10, 2015. E-mail correspondence with author, July 11–October 6, 2015.

Watson, Rubie S. "Girls' Houses and Working Women." In *Women and Chinese Patriarchy: Submission, Servitude, and Escape*, edited by Maria Jaschok and Suzanne Miers. London and Atlantic Highlands, NJ: Zed Books, 1994.

Florence Eastman Williams

Clough, Stan. "Zion Upon a Hill: Portland's AME Zion Church and Social Uplift in the Progressive Era." MA thesis, University of Southern Maine, 1994.

Hoose, Shoshana, and Karine Oldin, producers. *Anchor of the Soul: The History of an African-American Community in Portland, Maine*. Documentary video, 1994.

McKenzie, June. Interviews by author, Portland, Maine, September 17, October 7, and November 9, 2004, and January 5, 2005.

McKenzie, Merita. "Unpublished reminiscence of her grandmother, Florence Eastman Williams." December 2004.

McKenzie, Michele. Telephone interview by author, November 14, 2004.

Price, H. H. "African American Settlements Crucial to Underground Railroad." *Maine Archives and Museums Newsletter*, February 1998, 3–4.

———. "Maine Is on National Underground Railroad." *Maine Archives and Museums Newsletter*, November 1997, 1, 16.

Rogers, Phyllis. Interview by author, Portland, Maine, October 18, 2004.

Sister R. Mildred Barker

Barker, Sister R. Mildred. *The Sabbathday Lake Shakers: An Introduction to the Shaker Heritage*. Sabbathday Lake, ME: Shaker Press, 1985.

Burns, Ken, director. *The Shakers: Hands to Work, Hearts to God*. Florentine Films, 1984. PBS, 1985.

Carr, Sister Frances A. *Growing Up Shaker*. Sabbathday Lake, ME: United Society of Shakers, 1994.

Davenport, Tom, director. *The Shakers*. Davenport Films, 1974.

Newman, Cathy. "The Shakers' Brief Eternity." *National Geographic* 176, no. 3 (September 1989).

Sabbathday Lake Shaker Village. "Historical Background." http://maineshakers.com/history.

Wertkin, Gerard C. *The Four Seasons of Shaker Life* (photographs). New York: Simon and Schuster, 1986.

Margaret Chase Smith

Margaret Chase Smith Center for Public Policy. "Biography: Margaret Chase Smith." www.umaine.edu/mcsc/AboutUs/Bio.htm.

Margaret Chase Smith Library. "Expanded Biography." www.mcslibrary.org/bio/biolong.htm.

National Women's Hall of Fame. "Margaret Chase Smith." https://www.womenofthe hall.org/inductee/margaret-chase-smith.

Schmidt, Patricia L. *Margaret Chase Smith: Beyond Convention*. Orono: University of Maine Press, 1996.

Sherman, Janann. *No Place for a Woman: A Life of Senator Margaret Chase Smith*. New Brunswick, NJ: Rutgers University Press, 2000.

Stockwell, Angela N., Herbert E. Paradis Jr., and Virginia Foster, comps. and eds. *What Can I Do for You: Margaret Chase Smith's Story*. Skowhegan, ME: Central Maine Printing and Publishing, 1997.

Wallace, Patricia Ward. *Politics of Conscience: A Biography of Margaret Chase Smith*. Westport, CT: Praeger, 1995.

Marguerite Yourcenar

Acocella, Joan. "Becoming the Emperor." *The New Yorker*, February 14 and 21, 2005, 242–51.

Bernier, Yvon. *Petite Plaisance: Marguerite Yourcenar, 1903–1987*. Northeast Harbor, ME: Petite Plaisance Trust, 1994.

Bushell, Agnes. "Petite Plaisance." *Down East: The Magazine of Maine*, July 1999, 80–82, 105–7.

Howard, Joan E. Guided tour of Petite Plaisance, Northeast Harbor, Maine, August 6, 2015.

Savigneau, Josyane. *Marguerite Yourcenar: Inventing a Life*. Translated by Joan E. Howard. Chicago and London: University of Chicago Press, 1993. Originally published as *Marguerite Yourcenar: L'Invention d'une vie* (Paris: Éditions Gallimard, 1990).

Trustman, Deborah. "France's First Woman 'Immortal.'" *New York Times Magazine*, January 18, 1981, 18–22, 42, 44.

Yourcenar, Marguerite. *The Abyss*. Translated by Grace Frick. New York: Farrar, Straus and Giroux, 1976. Originally published as *L'Œuvre au Noir* (Paris: Éditions Gallimard, 1968).

——. *Memoirs of Hadrian*. Translated by Grace Frick. New York: Farrar, Straus and Giroux. 1963. Originally published as *Mémoires d'Hadrien* (Paris: Librairie Plon, 1951).

——. *With Open Eyes: Conversations with Matthieu Galey*. Translated by Arthur Goldhammer. Boston: Beacon Press, 1984. Originally published as *Les yeux ouverts: Entretiens avec Matthieu Galey* (Paris: Éditions Centurions, 1980).

INDEX

INDEX

INDEX

ACKNOWLEDGMENTS

Many thanks to the staff of the Maine Women Writers Collection and the librarians at the University of New England, and to the Maine Historical Society for your resources, patience, and enthusiasm, and especially to Gary Libby, lawyer and historian of the Chinese in Maine, whose fine storytelling convinced me to write about the life of Toy Len Goon. I'm very grateful to Toy Len's family, daughter Doris Wong, daughter-in-law Amy Guen, and grandson Leo T. Guen, for animating her fascinating past and offering thoughtful edits over multiple drafts.

Thank you to Joan E. Howard, Marguerite Yourcenar scholar, for your wonderful tour of Petite Plaisance, Madame Yourcenar's house on Mount Desert Island, and for your expert, thoughtful, and well-informed comments on my chapter.

For help with individual chapters from the first edition, I'm grateful to writers, historians, and family members who have shared their insights, photos, and sometimes memories of the women presented here: Geraldine Chassé, Rhéa Côté Robbins, March O. McCubrey, Charles N. Shay, Emma Nicolar, Caron Shay, Bunny McBride, Dahlov Ipcar, Bob Ipcar, Peggy Zorach, Jessica Nicoll, June McKenzie, Michele McKenzie, Merita McKenzie, Phyllis Rogers, and the Sabbathday Lake Society of Shakers and its library staff.

Thank you, Courtney Oppel, at Globe Pequot, for your topnotch editing.

Daily gratitude goes to my kind, stalwart, inspiring friends, Eleanor Morse, Cathy Wright, Agnes Bushell, and Mary Cushman, and to

extended family, especially the three amazing generations of Kennedy/
Greene/Burke/Hiller/Ray/Moreno/Williamson/Abel/Vidor girls and
women. And thank you, Rachel Kennedy Greene, matriarch-in-training,
and Nate Greene, for thirty-five years of love, laughter, and life support.

ABOUT THE AUTHOR

Kate Kennedy, writer, teacher, and literary coach, was the director of the Southern Maine Writing Project at the University of Southern Maine from 2006 to 2012. She taught writing half-time at Portland High School for twenty years and has also taught English as a Second Language (ESL) to adults, basic literacy, and Sudden Fiction. In 2001, her novel, *End Over End*, was published by Soho Press. Her short fiction has appeared in various small magazines, her nonfiction in *The Island Journal* and *Arts Everyday*. Other projects include writing a library discussion guide for WGBH-Masterpiece Theatre and editing the Maine Island Trail Association's annual guidebook. Although she grew up in California and New Jersey, Maine has been Kate's home since 1977. She and her husband live in Cape Elizabeth, enjoying three generations of family within a sixty-five-mile span.